Startup Blueprints for Future Industry Leaders

13 STARTUP
Ideas For Sharks
Outside The Tank

Innovative Business Concepts for Aspiring Entrepreneurs
Navigating New Ventures Beyond the Pitch

INDARPAL UPPAL

BlueRose ONE
Stories Matter
NewDelhi • London

BLUEROSE PUBLISHERS
India | U.K.

Copyright © Indarpal Uppal 2024

All rights reserved by author. No part of this publication may be reproduced, stored in a retrieval system or transmitted in any form or by any means, electronic, mechanical, photocopying, recording or otherwise, without the prior permission of the author. Although every precaution has been taken to verify the accuracy of the information contained herein, the publisher assumes no responsibility for any errors or omissions. No liability is assumed for damages that may result from the use of information contained within.

BlueRose Publishers takes no responsibility for any damages, losses, or liabilities that may arise from the use or misuse of the information, products, or services provided in this publication.

BlueRose ONE
Stories Matter
NewDelhi • London

For permissions requests or inquiries regarding this publication, please contact:

BLUEROSE PUBLISHERS
www.BlueRoseONE.com
info@bluerosepublishers.com
+91 8882 898 898
+4407342408967

ISBN: 978-93-6452-625-8

Cover design: Tahira
Typesetting: Sagar

First Edition: October 2024

Acknowledgements

I am deeply grateful to my parents, Mr. G.S. Uppal and Mrs. Raj Kaur Uppal, whose blessings and upbringing have been the foundation of my journey. Your unwavering support and love have been my guiding light.

To my wife, Hetal, thank you for being my rock-solid support and strength. Your belief in me has been my greatest motivation, and I couldn't have done this without you.

A heartfelt thanks to my brother Hardeep Uppal and to my friends, Group Captain Nitin Jain (Retd), Mr. Rajeev Gulati, Bomy Talati, Anuya Amarnath, Jatin Hura, Sir Narendra Singh Khera, and Kalyani Sharma. Your encouragement, insights, and companionship have been invaluable in bringing this book to life. This accomplishment is as much yours as it is mine.

To my kids, Harpreet Uppal and Jaspreet Uppal, thank you for sharing your energy and passion for these ideas. You guys are superstars.

I also express my gratitude and devotion to God for guiding me throughout this project. Thank you for being part of this incredible journey.

Preface

In the fast-paced world of innovation, ideas can travel at lightning speed. This often leads many entrepreneurs to work on their concepts in secrecy, revealing them only when they are fully developed. However, it's not uncommon to find that despite having the resources, time, and expertise to launch, someone else has already brought a similar idea to market. This book aims to bridge that gap by providing entrepreneurs with a treasure trove of innovative ideas that are ready to be implemented.

Embark on a journey of transformation into the essence of innovation, sustainability and striving for a superior world. This book presents an opportunity to delve into start-up proposals that tackle urgent issues while also revolutionizing how we contemplate commerce, community and our surroundings. As you progress through these pages, prepare yourself for progressive ideas aimed at motivating, questioning and enabling you to catalyze change as an active participant.

Today, the need for sustainable and ethical business practices is more urgent than ever before. The rampant environmental degradation, social inequality, and unethical corporate conduct are critical issues that demand prompt action. However, these challenges present tremendous opportunities for imaginative visionaries who aspire to design viable solutions centered on promoting our planet's well-being while benefiting all living things in it. This book is an ode exclusively dedicated to those brave innovators eager to take up the baton of transformational change, a difference that counts now!

The book presents various innovative start-up ideas that effectively combine profitability, sustainability, and purpose, outlining ways companies can succeed while making a positive difference. Topics cover environmentally sustainable ventures addressing concerns such as climate change, depletion of resources, and pollution; social entrepreneurship with an emphasis on promoting equality, justice, and community advancement through business practices; plus, commerce strategies emphasizing ethical guidelines prioritizing transparency along with long-term value rather than short-term profits alone.

These start-up concepts go beyond theoretical musings, as they are actionable blueprints that can be adapted and implemented. They originate from the notion that creativity and entrepreneurship play a powerful role in solving intricate problems. The content provides thorough insights, practical strategies, and motivating examples showcasing how these ideas have the potential to create a tangible impact on societal change. Consider this book an open invitation to entrepreneurs who have the resources and time but are seeking fresh, actionable ideas. Feel free to adapt and execute these concepts without any worry about royalty payments – these ideas are shared freely for the benefit of all.

Beyond being a compilation of ideas, this book is an urgent appeal. We are convinced that every reader can play a part in advancing the movement - be it as an entrepreneur, investor, policymaker or advocate. Despite facing daunting challenges on our journey ahead towards sustainability and equality there is also enormous potential for innovation and change-making. Join us in making strides to implement these concepts into your sphere and work together with others toward creating a future characterized by longevity and fairness.

The content within these pages is the result of extensive research and data analysis. Each chapter presents a unique idea, allowing you to explore the book in any order that suits you. While some ideas may appear to overlap with existing start-ups, rest assured that each concept includes distinctive features and unique selling points that set them apart.

The last section of this book redirects our attention towards nineteen critical global concerns that often go unnoticed. Unlike the previous sections, it does not propose immediate remedies but instead motivates us to acknowledge these urgent predicaments and take action. This segment is a compelling appeal for readers like you to respond by initiating change; using the insights and motivation from this publication as fuel to launch your own transformative endeavors.

Even a single idea from this book could potentially be worth millions if executed wisely. Take it from Warren Buffett, the "Oracle of Omaha" and chairman of Berkshire Hathaway, who credits a book as the foundation of his multibillion-dollar empire. At the age of 19, Buffett purchased a copy of The Intelligent Investor by Benjamin Graham for just $1.30—a hardcover price in the early 1950s. He's often called it the best investment he ever made. Today, Buffett's net worth is $108.7 billion, after donating around $37 billion to charitable causes. Now that's what you call stellar ROI!

As you journey through this book, you will gain valuable insights into sustainable business ideas and their execution. By the end, you will be equipped with a wealth of knowledge and inspiration to embark on your entrepreneurial ventures. By uniting our efforts, we can transform ambitious concepts into concrete accomplishments. We can establish enterprises that not only prosper but also contribute positively to society. Join us on this adventure as we confront obstacles and capitalize on chances to effect a meaningful change in our world. I promise that this book will be a rewarding and enlightening experience.

This marks the start of an innovative age characterized by accountability - let's welcome it with open arms! The future is within reach; all we need to do is take action today.

Legal Disclaimer for the Book: "13 Start-up Ideas for Sharks Outside the Tank"

1. Introduction

The contents of this book, titled *13 Start-up Ideas for Sharks Outside the Tank* (hereafter referred to as "the Book"), are provided for informational and educational purposes only. By reading or using the content in the Book, you agree to the terms and conditions set forth in this Legal Disclaimer.

2. No Professional or Investment Advice

The ideas, opinions, and suggestions in the Book are based on the author's personal knowledge, experiences, and research. They do not constitute legal, financial, or investment advice. Readers are encouraged to seek professional advice from qualified individuals or entities before making any business or investment decisions. The author and publisher disclaim any liability, financial or otherwise, arising from the implementation or use of any idea, concept, or information provided in the Book.

3. No Warranties

The author and publisher make no representations or warranties, either express or implied, about the completeness, accuracy, reliability, suitability, or availability of the information contained in the Book. The information is provided on an "as-is" basis and is subject to change without notice.

4. Assumption of Risk

Readers assume all risks associated with the use of the information and ideas provided in the Book. The author and publisher shall not be liable for any damages, losses, or other liabilities that may arise from the use of the information provided, including but not limited to direct, indirect, consequential, or incidental damages.

5. No Endorsement

Any references to third-party businesses, organizations, or individuals mentioned in the Book are provided for informational purposes only. These references are not intended to imply endorsement, sponsorship, or recommendation by the author or publisher. The inclusion of such references does not constitute legal or investment advice.

6. Intellectual Property

All content in the Book, including but not limited to text, graphics, and illustrations, is protected by copyright law. Unauthorized use, reproduction, or distribution of any part of the Book is strictly prohibited. The author retains full copyright ownership of all material unless otherwise stated. The reader is not permitted to reproduce, modify, or distribute any part of the Book without prior written consent from the author.

7. Imaginary Brand Names

Any brand names, company names, or trademarks suggested or used in the Book are purely fictional and created for illustrative and educational purposes only. Any resemblance to existing brands or companies is purely coincidental. The inclusion of such names does not imply any affiliation with or endorsement by real-world companies.

8. Fictional Stories and Incidents

The Book may contain references to stories, incidents, or characters that are entirely fictitious and created for educational or illustrative purposes. Any resemblance to real persons, living or dead, or actual events is purely coincidental. The author has no intention of offending or targeting any group, belief, religion, or political ideology. If any such content is perceived as offensive, it is unintentional and the author offers an apology to those affected.

9. Third-Party Links

The Book may contain references or links to third-party websites or resources. The author and publisher do not assume any responsibility for the content or availability of these third-party resources. Readers who access such third-party content do so at their own risk.

10. Ideas and Suggestions

While the Book provides various startup ideas and business suggestions, it does not guarantee the success or viability of any particular idea. Market conditions, competition, and other factors play a significant role in the success of any business venture, and readers are encouraged to conduct thorough research and due diligence before proceeding with any business idea.

11. Disclaimer of Liability

To the fullest extent permitted by law, the author and publisher disclaim any liability or responsibility for any loss, damage, injury, or harm resulting from the reader's reliance on the information or ideas presented in the Book. This includes, but is not limited to, financial loss, business failure, or any other consequences of using the information provided.

12. No Legal Relationship

The use of this Book does not create an attorney-client or other professional relationship between the reader and the author or publisher. Any legal or financial questions should be directed to a qualified professional in the relevant field.

13. Governing Law

This Legal Disclaimer shall be governed by and construed in accordance with the laws and any disputes arising from this Disclaimer or the Book shall be subject to the exclusive jurisdiction of the courts of Ahmedabad.

14. Changes to the Disclaimer

The author and publisher reserve the right to amend or update this Legal Disclaimer at any time without prior notice. It is the reader's responsibility to review the disclaimer periodically for any changes.

Acknowledgment

By reading and using the Book, you acknowledge that you have read, understood, and agreed to the terms of this Legal Disclaimer.

Indarpal Uppal: A Visionary Leader in Sustainable Innovation

Indarpal Uppal is a seasoned business executive, entrepreneur, and startup investor with over 25 years of experience in the insurance and recycling sectors. As a passionate advocate for clean and sustainable energy solutions, Indarpal has dedicated his career to fostering environmentally responsible business practices.

As the Director of Greenfield Resources Private Limited, Indar is the CEO of a leading company in the textiles, plastics, and electronics recycling sector, where he is responsible for strategic planning, channel building, business development, and project management across India. His leadership has propelled Greenfield Resources to the forefront of the recycling industry, driving significant advancements in sustainability.

Indar's core competencies include identifying and seizing new business opportunities, cultivating and maintaining key account relationships, crafting and executing impactful marketing campaigns, and inspiring large teams to achieve unparalleled operational excellence. His mission is to leverage his expertise and network to create a positive impact on the environment and society through renewable energy.

Beyond his professional achievements, Indar is also a yoga enthusiast and has a passion for garba and traveling. His dedication to personal well-being and cultural pursuits enriches his perspective and fuels his drive for innovation.

With his maiden book, Indarpal Uppal shares his extensive knowledge and insights, aiming to empower investors and entrepreneurs to embrace sustainable startup ideas and drive meaningful change. Join him on this transformative journey towards a greener, more prosperous future.

The Ants and The Entrepreneur

Once upon a time, an entrepreneur, burdened with the weight of multiple failed ventures and a crippling debt, sought the counsel of a wise saint. Desperate and desolate, he confided in the saint, "I've failed in countless businesses, lost everything, and now I can't even feed my family. I'm at my wit's end and feel like giving up on life. Please help me."

The saint listened patiently and then spoke, "I will help you. Do you see that mountain over there? There's an old temple on top of that mountain, and nearby, thousands of ants reside. Surprisingly, these ants are damaging the soil and trees. Your task is to go to that mountain every day for seven days and destroy their homes. However, you must do this without harming a single ant."

Though confused by the saint's peculiar instruction, the entrepreneur agreed and returned home, pondering the odd task. The next day, he set out to the mountain and observed the ants diligently carrying food in a single line, building their homes. His heart softened at the sight of their hard work, but he remembered the saint's words and began demolishing their homes. The ants scattered in panic, and their homes lay in ruins.

The entrepreneur returned home, his heart heavy with guilt and sadness.

The following day, the entrepreneur returned to the mountain, only to find the ants had rebuilt their homes and were again gathering food. Astonished by their resilience, he demolished their homes once more, this time with added measures to prevent rebuilding. Yet, he couldn't help but question the morality of his actions and the saint's intentions.

On the third day, he was pleased to see no ant homes where he had previously demolished them. However, just as he was about to leave, he spotted new ant homes nearby. Realizing the saint foresaw this, he understood the lesson about persistence. He felt a deep empathy for the ants, remembering his own struggles. Despite his reluctance, he continued to destroy their homes carefully, ensuring no ants were harmed.

As days passed, the entrepreneur marveled at the ants' unwavering determination. Despite their homes being destroyed repeatedly, they rebuilt with renewed vigor. Their resilience mirrored his own entrepreneurial journey. Each day, he felt more conflicted, but continued his task, growing more introspective about his actions and the ants' incredible spirit.

By the seventh day, the entrepreneur could no longer bear to harm the ants. Instead, he brought food for them and watched in awe as they rebuilt their homes once more. He had learned a profound lesson from these tiny creatures. Returning to the saint, he confessed his failure to complete the task as instructed but felt he had learned something invaluable.

The saint, smiling, asked, "Why could you not destroy the ants' homes?"

The entrepreneur replied, "I did destroy their homes many times, even injuring some ants in the process. But each time, I realized how tirelessly they worked to rebuild. It felt wrong to harm them further. I saw their resilience, and it reminded me of my own failures and the need to keep trying despite them."

The saint nodded, "That is exactly the lesson I wanted you to learn. These ants, though small, possess a powerful will. They never give up, no matter how many times their homes are destroyed. From them, you learn that true strength lies in perseverance. Challenges will always be there, but giving up is never the answer."

He continued, "Remember, life tests us to see if we truly desire our goals. Just as the ants rebuilt their homes, you must rebuild your dreams. Keep trying, and the universe will conspire to help you succeed. Now, let me share with you 13 innovative startup ideas. If you pursue them with the same determination as those ants, you will surely succeed." THATAASTU!!!

With a newfound sense of purpose and a heart full of hope, the entrepreneur left the saint, ready to embrace his next venture with the resilience and determination of those tiny, unyielding ants.

Contents

Chapter-1
Cultivating Creativity: The "Reimagineer" App 1

Chapter -2
HEART SAVER: United Hearts, Unstoppable Impact
Keep Saving Lives, Keep Savoring Hearts!..22

Chapter-3
Swappo: The Bartering Revolution Empowering
Communities for Sustainable Trade.. 34

Chapter- 4
Celeb Connect: Learn with Stars 48

Chapter-5
Serenify Pods: Personalized Mental Wellness Pods................... 63

Chapter-6
SolarShare: Revolutionizing Energy Access
Through Community Sharing.. 85

Chapter-7
Redefining Sustainable Fashion with ReVerso.. 105

Chapter-8
Kinaya: Unveiling the Authentic Tapestry
of Asian Landscapes..117

Chapter-9
Revolutionizing Access to Affordable and
Accessible Healthcare: The Vision of Plansurge.com..........................139

Chapter-10
EmShe: Empowering Confidence - The Skillshare for
Women in STEM.. 153

Chapter- 11
Pawsitive Match: Revolutionizing the Search for
Your Furry (or Feathery) Friend.. 172

Chapter-12
Freshen Up: Cleanliness. Convenience. Comfort..................................... 185

Chapter-13
EcoValence: Nurturing a Sustainable Tomorrow................................... 202

Chapter-14
Plain Points 220

Chapter-1

Cultivating Creativity: The "Reimagineer" App

"Reimagineer," as the brand name, blends the terms "reimagine" and "engineer." It symbolizes both imaginative redesigning and technical expertise. The app reflects its purpose of fostering creativity by enabling users, particularly children, to reengineer ideas related to upcycling fashion while promoting ecological awareness. Thus, the name "Reimagineer" aptly represents the brand's mission toward sustainability—advocating for fashionable solutions by transforming outdated wardrobe items through innovative thinking.

Introduction

The fast fashion practices employed by the fashion industry have a significant impact on the environment, resulting in significant waste and environmental harm. This is further exacerbated by water scarcity which is projected to affect billions of people globally before 2050; thus, highlighting an urgent need for sustainable efforts worldwide. As such, several children's educational apps focus primarily on entertainment rather than offering meaningful learning experiences. To tackle these interrelated challenges creatively while promoting education and protecting our planet, "Reimagineer" emerges as a unique business idea that integrates creativity with sustainability initiatives and learning opportunities.

"Reimagineer" seeks to revolutionize the fashion and sustainability industry by providing a platform that promotes active engagement among children aged 8-12. By incorporating augmented reality (AR) and gamification, this innovative app encourages young users to creatively upcycle old clothing items in fun and creative ways. At the same time, it educates them on important topics like water conservation and sustainable practices. By cultivating an environmentally conscious mindset, "Reimagineer" aims to inspire future generations of thoughtful consumers committed to building a more sustainable world.

Market Research

Size & Potential

- The global fashion resale market is projected to reach 84.6 billion by 2026, indicating a strong demand for sustainable fashion options.

- Water scarcity is expected to affect 5 billion people by 2050, underscoring the urgent need for conservation efforts.

- According to Verified Market Reports, the global educational app market is expected to be worth USD 10.9 Billion by the end of 2030 with a CAGR of 10.2% during the forecast period of

2024-2030, highlighting the increasing need for engaging learning tools.

Uniqueness

"Reimagineer" uniquely combines these three sectors by gamifying the process of upcycling clothes, teaching kids about sustainability and water conservation in the process.

User Pain Points

- Parents struggle to find engaging educational apps that offer substantive learning experiences beyond passive entertainment.
- Consumers face limited options for sustainable and affordable clothing.
- The world needs innovative solutions to combat water waste and environmental damage.

Solution

"Reimagineer" is an educational app targeting children aged 8-12, turning the upcycling of clothes into a fun and rewarding experience. The app utilizes augmented reality (AR) to allow kids to see their designs virtually "worn" by different models, blending learning with play. It also includes educational modules that teach children about the environmental impact of fast fashion and the importance of water conservation, fostering a sense of responsibility and ecological awareness.

Functionality
- User Interface

The app features a user profile with an avatar and progress tracker, a design challenge section, learning module section, and a virtual closet showcasing completed designs. Additionally, the design studio allows users to select clothing, digitally embellish it and view their creations in AR mode, where the designs are virtually "worn" by models.

- Learning Modules

Interactive quizzes, games, animated videos, fun facts, trivia, and a "Clean Water Challenge" are the components of the learning modules, which create an engaging and informative learning environment.

Revenue Model & Social Impact

The revenue model follows a freemium approach, offering in-app purchases and partnerships with sustainable clothing brands and resale platforms. Users can access discounts and promotions; while a portion of the in-app revenue is donated to support environmental and water conservation initiatives, ensuring a sustainable business model with a positive social impact.

Deep Dive into Reimagineer: Cultivating Curiosity and Innovation Sparking Curiosity in Young Minds

"Reimagineer" ignites children's curiosity through the use of AR, gamification, empowerment and the discovery of sustainable practices, providing an engaging and impactful learning environment.

Functionality in Detail

The app's home screen, design studio, and learning modules, offer a comprehensive experience focused on upcycling, AR integration, and actionable lessons on sustainability. This holistic approach differentiates "Reimagineer" from the other existing educational apps.

Operating model of Reimagineer:

The "Reimagineer" app teaches children about sustainability through various engaging methods integrated into its functionality:

Gamified Upcycling Process: The app allows children to virtually upcycle clothes by adding digital embellishments, accessories, and patterns to outdated and pre-loved items. This hands-on activity fosters creativity and educates children about the concept of reusing and repurposing items, promoting sustainability practices like reducing waste.

Augmented Reality (AR) Integration: By using AR technology, children can see their designs virtually "worn" by different models in various settings. This feature provides a visual representation of their creative work, enhancing their understanding of how sustainable fashion choices can impact the overall look and feel of an outfit.

Educational Modules: The app includes interactive quizzes, games, animated videos, fun facts, and trivia about environmental impact of fast fashion and water scarcity. These learning modules present sustainability concepts in an engaging and entertaining way, making the learning process more enjoyable and effective for children.

"Clean Water Challenge": Children can earn points by completing design challenges and learning modules, which they can use to donate virtual "clean water kits" to communities in need. This feature allows children to see the direct impact of their choices, instilling a sense of social responsibility and showcasing the positive outcomes of environmentally conscious actions.

Empowerment and Agency: Beyond teaching theoretical knowledge, "Reimagineer" empowers children to become active participants in addressing real-world environmental problems.

Encouraging them to engage in virtual upcycling and sustainability initiatives within the app, cultivates a sense of agency and ownership for their environmental impact. Overall, the app uses a combination of interactive design activities, educational content, gamification, and direct social impact mechanisms to effectively teach children about sustainability, environmental conservation, and the importance of making eco-friendly choices.

Teaching sustainability beyond upcycling

The "Reimagineer" app educates children on sustainability, extending beyond just upcycling through various engaging and informative features:

- **Focus on Sustainable Choices**: In the design studio and virtual closet sections of the app, children can explore sustainable fabric options, eco-friendly embellishments, and design elements that promote environmentally conscious choices. By interacting with these features, they learn about the significance of selecting sustainable materials and the positive impact these choices have on the environment.

- **"Clean Water Challenge":** Through this feature, children earn points to donate virtual clean water kits to communities in need. The app raises awareness about water scarcity and the importance of conservation efforts. This hands-on activity allows children to understand the value of clean water and the impact of their actions on communities facing water challenges.

- **Environmental Impact Insights:** The app may incorporate hidden educational nuggets within the design elements or gameplay. For instance, clicking on sustainable fabric options could trigger pop-ups that provide information about their eco-friendly benefits. This subtle integration of sustainability education within the app's interactive features enhances children's knowledge of sustainable practices and their environmental impact.

By weaving educational content into the app's design and gameplay, "Reimagineer" offers a comprehensive approach to educating children about sustainability beyond just upcycling, it fosters values of environmental consciousness and responsible decision-making in young users.

Expanding the Reimagineer Universe:

Here are some ideas to further develop the "Reimagineer" app:

In-App Community and Social Features:

- Create a safe and moderated online community forum where kids can share their upcycled designs, inspire each other, and participate in design challenges together.

- Introduce a "leaderboard" system where users can earn points and badges for their upcycling efforts, learning achievements, and community contributions.

- Partner with sustainable fashion influencers or young climate activists to host virtual events or design contests within the app.

Gamification and Rewards:

- Implement a "Wardrobe Swap" feature where users can virtually trade pre-loved clothes with friends, promoting the concept of a circular fashion economy.

- Offer limited-edition digital decorations or AR filters as rewards for completing challenges or educational modules, increasing user engagement.

- Integrate a "Randomized Design Challenge" feature where users receive surprise prompts with specific themes or materials, encouraging creativity and adaptability.

Expanding Educational Content:

- Develop AR experiences that virtually demonstrate the environmental impact of the fashion industry in a visually compelling way. For example, users could virtually see the amount of water required to produce different fabrics.

- Partner with environmental organizations to offer educational content on broader sustainability issues like ethical sourcing, responsible consumerism, and waste reduction.

- Create a "Guest Speaker" series where kids can interact with virtual avatars of sustainability experts, learning about various aspects of environmental stewardship.

Monetization and Brand Partnerships:

- Partner with eco-friendly clothing brands to offer users exclusive discounts or promotions on sustainable clothing lines within the app.

- Integrate a "Donation Matching" feature where brands contribute to environmental causes when users make in-app purchases.

- Develop a subscription model offering premium features like access to exclusive design tools, AR filters and educational content.

Future Developments:

- Explore the use of AI technology to personalize the learning experience, by creating custom design challenges and educational modules tailored to user interests and progress.

- Develop an augmented reality "Shopping Experience" where users can virtually try on upcycled or sustainable clothing items before purchasing them in real life.
- Expand the app's functionality beyond clothing to encompass other upcycling projects, like electronic gadgets, toys, furniture or everyday household items.

By implementing these ideas, "Reimagineer" can evolve into a holistic platform that not only educates children but also empowers them to be change-makers in the fashion industry and advocates for a sustainable future.

Reimagineer: Cultivating Creativity and Expanding Horizons

Global Citizenship and Cultural Awareness:

- **"Reimagineer the World" Challenge:** Introduce design challenges that incorporate cultural elements from around the globe. Kids can virtually upcycle clothes with traditional patterns, accessories, or motifs, fostering cultural appreciation and understanding.
- **Partner with international schools or NGOs:** Collaborate with educational institutions or organizations working with underprivileged communities. Kids can use the app to design virtual clothing donations specifically for children in those communities.

Real-World Impact and Experiential Learning:

- **"Clean Clothes Closet" Initiative:** Partner with local thrift stores or donation centres to create a "Clean Clothes Closet" program. Kids can redeem points earned in the app for vouchers to purchase pre-loved clothing, reinforcing the connection between virtual and real-world sustainability efforts.

- **AR Scavenger Hunts:** Introduce location-based AR scavenger hunts where kids can explore their surroundings in search of sustainable or recycled fashion items in local shops or vintage stores. This encourages them to actively seek out sustainable fashion options in their communities.

Personalization and Skill Development:

- **Style Quizzes and Recommendations:** Integrate a fun style quiz that recommends upcycling projects or design elements based on the user's preferences. This personalizes the experience and helps them develop their unique style identity.

- **Sewing and Upcycling Tutorials:** Offer basic sewing tutorials and upcycling techniques within the app, empowering children to bring their virtual designs to life. This fosters practical skills and encourages hands on learning.

Engaging Parents and Building a Family Experience:

- **"Family Design Studio" Feature:** Introduce a co-creation mode where parents and children can collaborate on design challenges. This fosters family bonding and encourages intergenerational discussions about sustainability.

- **Parent Dashboard and Progress Tracking:** Provide parents with a dashboard to track their child's progress, learning achievements, and environmental impact. This feature encourages parents to actively participate in their child's sustainability journey.

Additional Considerations:

- **Accessibility Features:** Ensure the app is accessible for children with disabilities by incorporating features like text-to-speech narration, closed captions for videos, and alternative input methods.
- **Offline Functionality:** Develop functionalities within the app that can be used offline, allowing children to continue designing and exploring even without an internet connection.

By incorporating these elements, Reimagineer can evolve from an app into a comprehensive platform for sustainable education, cultural exchange, and real-world impact. It can empower children to become not just informed consumers but also active participants in shaping a more sustainable future for fashion and the planet.

Reimagineer: Branching into the Future

Here are some futuristic ideas to propel Reimagineer beyond the realm of a mobile app:

AR Fashion Shows and Virtual Reality Experiences:

- **Live "Reimagineer Runway" Events:** Host live, virtual fashion shows where kids showcase their upcycled designs in an immersive AR environment. This could involve creating digital avatars that wear the user's designs or utilizing AR technology to project the designs onto real models.

- **VR Upcycling Workshops:** Develop virtual reality workshops where kids can explore different upcycling techniques in a 3D space. They could virtually experiment with disassembling clothes, applying embellishments, and seeing the final product come to life in a realistic setting.

AI-Powered Design Assistant and Personalized Learning:

- **"Reimagineer AI" Assistant:** Introduce an AI-powered design assistant that suggests upcycling ideas, fabric combinations, and embellishments based on the user's preferences and existing wardrobe. This personalized approach enhances creativity and streamlines the design process.

- **Adaptive Learning Modules:** Use AI to personalize the learning modules based on the child's progress and interests. The app can adapt the difficulty level, suggest relevant content, and focus on areas where the child needs improvement, creating a more efficient and engaging learning experience.

Expanding Reimagineer's Reach:

- **Educational Licensing for Schools:** Develop a licensing program for schools, allowing educators to integrate Reimagineer into their sustainability curriculum. This could involve pre-designed lesson plans, interactive activities within the app, and progress-tracking tools for teachers.

- **"Reimagineer Maker Kits":** Create physical maker kits that complement the app. These kits could include pre-loved clothing scraps, sustainable embellishments, and basic sewing tools, allowing kids to translate their virtual creations into tangible upcycled garments.

Sustainability Gamification Beyond the App:

- **"Reimagineer Challenges" in Real Life:** Partner with local businesses and organizations to host real-world Reimagineer challenges. These could include upcycling workshops, clothing swaps, or community clean-up events, extending the app's impact beyond the virtual sphere.

- **"Reimagineer Points for Real Rewards":** Allow kids to earn points within the app that can be redeemed for real-world rewards related to sustainability. These could include discounts at eco-friendly stores, coupons for sustainable clothing brands, or even donations to environmental causes on their behalf.

Reimagineer: Cultivating Creativity for a Sustainable Future (Advanced Concepts)

Here are some advanced ideas to push the boundaries of the Reimagineer concept:

Immersive Learning and Gamification:

- **Biomimicry Design Challenges:** Introduce design challenges inspired by nature. Kids can use the app to create virtually upcycled clothes with patterns or textures that mimic animal adaptations, like camouflage or bioluminescence. This would foster an appreciation for nature's ingenuity and inspire sustainable design solutions.

- **AR "Eco-Impact Simulator":** Develop an AR simulation that allows kids to see the environmental footprint of different clothing choices. By virtually "wearing" different garments, they can see the water usage, carbon emissions, and waste generated by each piece in their production cycle. This creates a powerful visual representation of sustainable fashion choices.

- **Gamified Supply Chain Exploration:** Introduce a gamified experience where kids embark on a virtual journey through the clothing supply chain. They can learn about the different stages of production, sourcing of materials, and the impact of each step on the environment, fostering a deeper understanding of sustainable practices.

AI and Personalization on a New Level:

- **AI-Powered Style Evolution:** Utilize AI to track a child's design preferences and create a personalized "Style Profile" that evolves over time. The app can suggest upcycling projects and design elements that align with the child's developing fashion sense, while still promoting sustainable choices.

- **"Reimagineer Swap & Stitch":** Develop a feature that utilizes AI image recognition to suggest upcycling projects based on existing clothing items in a user's closet. Kids can virtually "swap" elements from different garments and explore potential upcycling combinations before starting a physical project.

Expanding Reimagineer's Ecosystem:

- **Reimagineer Marketplace:** Create a virtual marketplace where kids can sell their upcycled designs as digital fashion items for avatars in popular online games or virtual worlds. This fosters entrepreneurship, encourages peer-to-peer learning, and introduces the concept of a circular fashion economy within the digital realm.

- **"Rewear Reality" Integration:** Partner with social media platforms to develop an "AR clothing filter" named "Rewear Reality." This filter would allow users to virtually "upcycle" their existing clothes in photos or videos, promoting sustainable fashion choices beyond the app and encouraging social sharing.

Sustainability Beyond Fashion:

- **Reimagineer for Everyday Objects:** Expand the app's functionality beyond clothing to encompass upcycling projects for everyday household items. Kids could design virtual makeovers for furniture, toys, or other objects, promoting a culture of repair and resourcefulness.

- **"Reimagineer City Challenges":** Partner with municipalities to create location-based "Reimagineer City Challenges." Kids can use the app to identify areas for sustainable improvement in their communities, propose virtual upcycling projects for public spaces, and raise awareness about local environmental issues.

USP (Unique Selling Points)

The unique selling points (USPs) of the Reimagineer app:

- **Combines education, gamification and entertainment:** Reimagineer teaches kids about sustainability and upcycling through a fun and engaging app that combines educational modules with gamified elements and an entertaining design studio.

- **Focuses on upcycling clothes:** Unlike other educational apps that focus on general sustainability topics, Reimagineer specifically targets the fashion industry and teaches kids about upcycling clothes, promoting a more circular fashion economy.

- **Uses augmented reality (AR) to visualize designs:** Reimagineer utilizes AR technology to allow kids to see their upcycled designs virtually "worn" by different models, providing a more realistic and engaging experience.

- **Empowers kids to take action:** The app goes beyond just teaching kids about sustainability; it empowers them to take action through features like the "Clean Water Challenge" and the ability to earn points for completing design challenges and learning modules.

- **Has a social and environmental impact:** Reimagineer has a positive social and environmental impact by promoting sustainable fashion choices, reducing textile waste, and fostering a sense of environmental responsibility in children.

- **Offers in-app purchases and brand partnerships for a sustainable business model:** The freemium model with in-app purchases and brand partnerships ensures the app's financial sustainability while also allowing it to donate a portion of its revenue to support environmental and water conservation initiatives.

Maya and the App that Changed the World: A Reimagineer Story

Maya, a bright-eyed 10-year-old with a passion for fashion, scrolled through her tablet, bored with the usual games. Her older brother, Leo, noticed her frown. "What's wrong, Maya?"

"Everything's the same old, same old," Maya sighed. "These games are boring, and none of them teach me anything new."

Leo, a tech whiz himself, grinned. " I found this cool app called Reimagineer. It's like a fashion studio and a game all rolled into one, but the best part is, it teaches you about taking care of the planet!"

Intrigued, Maya downloaded the app. A spunky animated avatar named "Refashion Riley" greeted her. Riley explained how Reimagineer could turn old clothes into amazing new outfits through upcycling. Maya scanned an old t-shirt with a faded superhero logo. On the screen, the shirt transformed! She could add sparkly appliques, and neon paint splatters, and even virtually try it on different models in various settings.

As Maya designed, Riley popped up with fun facts about the environmental impact of the fashion industry. Maya learned about the water wasted to make new clothes and the mountains of textiles discarded each year. She felt a spark of determination. "We can do better than that," she declared.

By completing design challenges, Maya earned points and unlocked the "Clean Water Challenge." Here, she could donate virtual "clean water kits" to communities in need. Every time she upcycled an old shirt or pair of jeans, she felt a sense of accomplishment – she wasn't just creating cool clothes, she was helping the planet too!

One day, a new challenge popped up: the "Reimagineer the World" contest. Kids from all over the globe were invited to design outfits inspired by different cultures. Maya poured her heart into it, creating a vibrant dress with a traditional Indian print she'd learned about in school. To her surprise, her design won! As a reward, Reimagineer partnered with a sustainable clothing brand to turn her virtual creation into a real dress which was donated to a school in India.

Maya's journey with Reimagineer had just begun. She started a club at school, teaching her friends about upcycling and the app. They even organized a clothing swap, giving pre-loved clothes a new lease on life. Maya, once a bored gamer, had become a sustainability champion, inspiring others to take action, one upcycled outfit at a time.

These advanced concepts push Reimagineer's boundaries, creating a more immersive, personalized, and impactful experience for users. By embracing new technologies and fostering a global community of young sustainability advocates, Reimagineer can become a powerful force for positive change in the fashion industry and beyond.

Conclusion

"Reimagineer" is a unique and innovative educational app that not only educates children about sustainability but also empowers them to become active participants in solving real-world problems. The app aims to cultivate a generation of responsible consumers and innovators dedicated to a more sustainable future, setting new standards for educational apps while promoting eco-consciousness in the fashion industry.

Chapter -2

HEART SAVER: United Hearts, Unstoppable Impact. Keep Saving Lives, Keep Savoring Hearts!

Introduction

Our vision is perfectly embodied by the name "Heart Saver", as it succinctly communicates our unwavering dedication to supplying urgent, life-saving assistance during cardiac emergencies. This name symbolizes our obligation to save lives through prompt and effective measures while cultivating a pool of skilled responders who are poised for action when every second counts.

Consider this: According to a WHO report, Cardiovascular Diseases (CVDs) are claiming an astounding 17.9 million lives annually worldwide, leaving a trail of heartbreak and sorrow. This figure is projected to rise to 23 million by 2030. In the face of this global health crisis, India shoulders a staggering 60% of the burden, struggling with a surge in heart attack incidents. Shockingly, heart attack-related deaths in India have seen a surge by a spine-chilling 22% between 2017 and 2022. But that's not all—India has also been labeled the "diabetes capital of the world" with a staggering 101 million diabetics and 136 million prediabetics in urgent need of preventive measures. It's a dual crisis—diabetes and heart disease going hand in hand.

Amidst these grave statistics, there is an urgent need for a transformative solution that can bridge the gap between life and death during cardiac emergencies. Enter a visionary idea—building a robust community of real-life heroes, specially trained to become saviors of hearts—**Hriday Rakshaks!** Introducing "**Heart Saver**," the app designed to create a network of life-saving champions, armed with the power of Cardiopulmonary Resuscitation (CPR).

You might wonder, "How can an app change the game in a life-or-death situation?" Well, the Heart Saver app engages and certifies individuals as Hriday Rakshaks through accredited institutes, equipping them with the proficiency to perform CPR with precision. In times of crisis, a person experiencing a heart attack can activate the app's emergency button, immediately alerting nearby Hriday Rakshaks. Swiftly summoned to the scene, these trained saviors can administer critical first aid in the form of CPR, potentially turning the tide between life and death.

Let's dive into the incredible world of **Heart Saver** and explore its amazing features, the genius execution methods, and even sneak a peek into the revenue models that would keep this life-saving app ticking. But more importantly, we will highlight the tremendous social impact this app could have, positioning Heart

Saver as a game changer, saving lives while combating the growing threat of heart disease.

Pain Points

Despite significant advancements in medical science, including better techniques and knowledge of preventive measures, cardiovascular diseases remain a formidable global health challenge. Conditions such as heart attacks, cardiac arrests, and other related issues, strike unpredictably, affecting people of all ages and backgrounds.

Moreover, the COVID-19 pandemic has cast a haunting shadow on the health landscape, not only affecting respiratory health but also exacerbating cardiovascular issues. In India, the post-pandemic period has witnessed a distressing surge in cases of cardiac arrests and heart attacks. Amidst this unsettling rise, a critical pain point emerges—i.e. the lack of early diagnosis and widespread unawareness regarding life-saving Cardiopulmonary Resuscitation (CPR) procedures during emergencies.

Here are a few real-life incidents related to cardiac arrest, highlighting the dire need for a solution that can provide immediate assistance for individuals with cardiovascular diseases.

Incident 1: The Unyielding Heart

In the vibrant city of Jamnagar, Gujarat, lived a remarkable soul, Dr. Gandhi, a renowned Cardiologist. His hands, skilled and steady, had performed over

16,000 heart surgeries, earning him admiration and accolades from patients and peers alike. On the occasion of India's Republic Day, he was honored for his unparalleled service and groundbreaking research in the medical field. Beyond his profession, Dr. Gandhi lived life with zest, enjoying cricket and fitness, and was a regular at the local gym.

The esteemed doctor was known for his boundless energy and unwavering dedication. Little did anyone know that amidst his tireless efforts to mend broken hearts, an unexpected twist of fate awaited him. One fateful day, the news spread like wildfire—Dr. Gandhi had suffered a cardiac arrest and passed away.

The very expert who had saved countless lives succumbed to the condition that he had fought to conquer. His tragic demise was a stark reminder of the need to address cardiovascular emergencies with swiftness and precision, igniting a determination to create a world where everyone is ready to respond, a world envisioned by **"Heart Saver"**.

Incident 2: The Silent Departure

In a quiet neighborhood, Mr. Akaash Sharma, a genial and vibrant man in his early fifties, lived a content life free of any medical worries. One evening, after returning from work, he mentioned some minor chest discomfort to his wife. Unperturbed, they enjoyed dinner together, unaware that this evening would forever change their lives. As Mr. Sharma retired to bed, his wife noticed a strange stillness in the room moments later. Panic ensued as she realized something was terribly wrong. She desperately sought help, and neighbors rushed to their aid, including a doctor from the society. Despite their swift attempts, they couldn't reverse the tragedy—the heart attack had claimed Mr. Sharma's life. This heart-wrenching incident highlighted the critical need for CPR awareness and prompt intervention during such emergencies.

Incident 3: A Savior on Two Wheels

On a bustling street near Kalupur Circle in Ahmedabad, life took an unexpected turn for a young man on his Honda Activa bike. Suddenly, he collapsed, gasping for breath. Fate smiled upon him as two traffic police officers, displaying a blend of professionalism and humanity, rushed to his aid. Recognizing the urgency, they immediately initiated CPR. Their life-saving skills became a beacon of hope. Emergency services were summoned, and an ambulance promptly arrived, whisking the young man to the hospital. Thanks to the timely actions and CPR expertise of the officers, a life was saved, reinforcing the significance of CPR knowledge among ordinary individuals.

Incident 4: The Playground's Sorrow

The school playground echoed with laughter as children played a spirited game of cricket. Among them was a bright-eyed young boy, his dreams soaring high like a kite. Suddenly, the cheers faded into a stumped silence as the boy collapsed, clutching his chest. The playground, once a symbol of joy, was now shrouded in sorrow. Despite immediate efforts, the tragic outcome was unavoidable, leaving behind a heartbroken community. This devastating incident underscored the vulnerability of young hearts and the need for CPR awareness in educational institutions, potentially saving lives in moments of crisis.

Incident 5: The Dance of Tragedy

In the midst of a festive celebration, vibrant colors swirled around as the community indulged in the joyous Garba dance. Amidst the revelry, one participant's energetic steps faltered, unnoticed by the crowd. As the dance continued, the individual collapsed, their heart faltering with each beat. The joyous gathering quickly turned into a scene of shock and panic. Despite immediate medical attention, the person could not be revived. The incident served as a poignant reminder of the importance of cardiac health awareness, especially during communal gatherings where early CPR intervention could make a life-saving difference.

Addressing this critical gap and empowering the communities to become proactive in tackling cardiac emergencies is the central mission of **"Heart Saver"** app. By fostering a network of certified Hriday Rakshaks (Heart Saviors) equipped with CPR skills, the app endeavors to create a united front against deadly cardiovascular diseases. Through user-friendly features and innovative execution, Heart Saver seeks to bridge the gap between those in need and life-saving assistance, reshaping the narrative of cardiac emergencies in India and beyond.

In the forthcoming sections, we will delve into the key functionalities of the Heart Saver app, exploring its various features and execution methodologies.

Functionality and Execution Methodologies

Life-Saving Mode

In a world where a few precious seconds can mean the difference between life and death, the **"Heart Saver"** app's Life-Saving Mode emerges as a crucial beacon of hope. When users face symptoms of a heart attack or a cardiac arrest, they simply need to press the emergency button on the app. At this moment, the app's AI quickly locates and alerts nearby Hriday Rakshaks (Heart Saviors) within the radius. These specifically trained individuals, comprising of a diverse community of points of contact ranging from gym instructors, teachers, security staff, and more, are immediately alerted. The first Rakshak to respond is connected with the patient, confirming their acceptance to render life-saving assistance.

During this critical waiting period, the app provides crucial information, such as the estimated time and distance for the Hriday Rakshak to arrive. In the event that multiple Rakshaks respond, the app coordinates to ensure a prompt and effective intervention. Additionally, 108 Ambulance services are also alerted, ensuring arrival of professional medical assistance.

To ensure that maximum citizens are trained in CPR, the app collaborates with doctors, other medical professionals, and certified trainers who possess comprehensive knowledge of CPR. They impart essential training to the Hriday Rakshaks, empowering them with life-saving skills. Beyond medical care staff, the app encourages the inclusion of CPR training in schools, colleges, and various institutions to create a community that is well-prepared for emergencies.

Training Mode

Recognizing the significance of widespread CPR knowledge, the "Heart Saver" app features a dedicated Training Mode. Users can easily scroll through a curated list of available trainers, each with their credentials and expertise published. Once a preferred trainer has been selected, users can then confirm the number of participants for the training session and choose suitable batch timings. Payment for the training sessions can be made conveniently through the app's secure payment gateways.

The responsibility of sponsoring CPR training lies with the principals and employers, who ensure that key employees in organizations receive this life-saving education. Similarly, schools are responsible for training students, and residential and commercial establishments, led by management committees must ensure that their members are equipped with these essential skills. Self-employed professionals are encouraged to take the initiative to sponsor their own

CPR training, thereby contributing to a safer and more prepared society.

A Safer World, A Priceless Gift!

With the **"Heart Saver"** app, by making a few minutes of mandatory CPR training a priority for key points of contact, we can significantly increase survival rates in cardiac emergencies. To further promote preventive healthcare, the app advocates for mandatory CT Coronary Angiography screenings for adults over the age of 40. Life and General Insurance companies can play their part by offering free/discounted screening as an incentive to their clients during premium renewals or through discount offers. These preventive measures are essential in safeguarding lives and promoting a greater peace of mind.

Expanding Scope

The potential of the "Heart Saver" app extends beyond cardiovascular emergencies. It can be adapted to address other medical crises such as strokes, accidents, dizziness, fire burns, and accidental falls. By triggering alerts to emergency ambulance services like 108, the app ensures rapid responses to various critical situations, thus transforming into a comprehensive life-saving platform.

The **"Heart Saver"** app will stand as a testament to human solidarity—a digital lifeline connecting hearts and uniting us in the mission to save lives.

Revenue Model

Commercial Scope

- **Training Program Revenue:** To build a network of skilled Hriday Rakshaks, the app enrolls doctors and trainers who offer CPR training to groups of individuals. Corporates, educational institutions, and society management committees can sponsor these training programs. The app will charge a fee for the training, and a portion of the revenue will be shared with the trainers.

- **Insurance Company Integration:** The "Heart Saver" app can partner with General and Life Insurance companies, integrating its API into their policies. These insurers can then offer CPR training as a value-added service to their clients, promoting preventive healthcare and enhancing their service offerings while supporting a social cause.

- **Commission from Healthcare Partners:** The app can establish partnerships with hospitals and diagnostic centres to promote preventive measures, such as CT Coronary Angiography tests and other health checkups. For every test or service facilitated through the app, the platform earns a commission. By fostering a culture of proactive healthcare, "Heart Saver" contributes to early detection and timely interventions for potential heart-related issues.

- **App Downloads:** Once the app achieves popularity and garners a substantial user base, it can introduce a nominal download fee for new users, such as Rs 99 per user. This ensures sustainability and enables further expansion of the app's outreach.

Social Scope

Grants and CSR Funds: Emphasizing its social impact, the "Heart Saver" app can seek financial support through government grants and Corporate Social Responsibility (CSR) funds from businesses. These funds can become essential for the app to reach diverse communities, particularly underserved regions where access to life-saving interventions is limited and can be instrumental

The **"Heart Saver"** app strikes a harmonious balance between its commercial scope and social mission. By generating revenue through strategic partnerships and user engagement, the app ensures sustainable growth while remaining committed to its core purpose of creating a community equipped to save lives during cardiac emergencies. As we venture into the next phase, the fusion of commercial and social elements in the app's revenue model showcases the true essence of entrepreneurship with a profound impact on society.

Social Impact: A Heartfelt Revolution

The advent of the **"Heart Saver"** app heralds a transformative shift in how society addresses cardiovascular emergencies. By fostering a community of Hriday Rakshaks armed with life-saving CPR skills, the app empowers ordinary individuals to become guardians of life. The ripple effect of this initiative extends far beyond healthcare. Families are reassured knowing that their loved ones are surrounded by a vigilant network of compassionate souls ready to respond in moments of crisis. Educational institutions instill CPR training in their curriculum, creating a generation of young hearts trained to save lives. Corporates and organizations embrace preventive healthcare, investing in the well-being of their employees and communities. Insurance companies embrace a holistic approach, rewarding clients with CPR training as a testament to their commitment to societal welfare. The **"Heart Saver"** app illuminates a path towards a safer, more resilient society, where every heartbeat resonates with the potential to rescue, restore, and cherish life.

Conclusion: Embracing the Heart Saver's Promise

The **"Heart Saver"** app stands as a testament to the power of human ingenuity and compassion. United in our shared pursuit of a safer tomorrow, this transformative startup embodies a unique fusion of technology with empathy, and commerce with social responsibility. By aligning its commercial goals with the noble cause of saving lives, we have unlocked a virtuous cycle where revenue sustains the heart of our mission: empowering communities to respond with courage, grace, and skill in the face of cardiac emergencies. As the chapters of this unique startup unfold, let us embrace the promise of the **"Heart Saver" app**—a promise that transcends boundaries, redefines heroism, and weaves together the fabric of hope.

Chapter-3

Swappo: The Bartering Revolution Empowering Communities for Sustainable Trade

Introduction

"Swappo's name originates from the core principle of exchanging skills and products in a modern, streamlined environment. It embodies an agile, user-friendly platform that enables effortless bartering. The imaginative take on the word "swap" emphasizes Swappo's progressive and captivating nature - presenting it as a groundbreaking method for sharing expertise by means of exchange."

In this chapter, we will explore an intriguing concept derived from e-commerce services: a focus on the Barter System as a trade mechanism. **Sounds Interesting?** Let's dive into the exciting world of **Swappo**, an online platform designed to connect users, allowing them to exchange goods and services within their community. Swappo addresses a significant gap in the market by providing a streamlined and efficient solution to the challenge of managing excess possessions and finding sustainable alternatives to traditional buying and selling.

Every few days, people face the overwhelming task of de-cluttering their homes to make space for new items. For instance, the average American home houses around 300,000 items, ultimately leading to stress and disarray. The rise of e-commerce has further fueled this trend, with more items being purchased and stored than ever before. Amidst this abundance, there is a pressing need for a dedicated platform that enables individuals to exchange their possessions and services, fostering a sense of community and promoting sustainable consumption.

While several online marketplaces exist for buying and selling used products, the concept of bartering and swapping has been largely overlooked. The thrill of exchanging goods and services, finding mutually beneficial agreements, and discovering hidden treasures has been confined to the limited scope of physical flea markets. But what if there was a digital platform that seamlessly facilitated skill swapping, product exchanging and even a combination of both (product-skill swapping) by connecting people with complimentary needs and interests? **Enter Swappo.**

Swappo offers a user-friendly and intuitive interface that allows individuals to list their items and services for exchange. Unlike traditional marketplaces, Swappo introduces an innovative approach: exchange requests are only published when a corresponding request to buy is published, ensuring a balanced and fair bartering experience. This unique feature sets Swappo apart, making it a go-to platform for those seeking to swap their possessions for something they truly desire.

Swappo is powered by advanced AI algorithms, which match product listings with users' intended exchanges, taking into account budgetary constraints. This intelligent matching system provides users with a curated list of items they might be interested in swapping. However, Swappo goes beyond mere bartering, offering options of donating items to Non-Profit Organizations (NPOs) or dispose of them responsibly through authorized recyclers, promoting social impact and environmental consciousness.

In the upcoming sections of this chapter, we will explore the difficulties experienced by individuals in the absence of a dedicated bartering platform. We will discuss Swappo's execution strategies and analyze its revenue models for sustainability. Moreover, we will delve into the social impact that Swappo can bring when it becomes available to the public, transforming the way we exchange goods and services within our communities.

Virtual Reality Bartering

Imagine stepping into a digital marketplace where proficiency and know-how replace traditional currency. This is the heart of the innovative Virtual Reality (VR) Barter System, enabling individuals to trade their abilities in real time. Whether you seek guidance from an expert potter or offer culinary aptitude in exchange, this platform fosters interactive skill swapping that transcends conventional bartering methods for a truly immersive experience.

The VR Barter System is a creative solution facilitating global networking, surpassing physical barriers to exchange expertise in technical areas like coding, photography, pottery, cooking, gardening, fitness, music etc. By using realistic virtual platforms for live exchanges, individuals can engage in hands-on skill-sharing while forming meaningful connections along the way. The value of this system lies not only in the increased accessibility to education but also in an enjoyable and customized learning experience enhanced by active participation within the community.

Utilizing state-of-the-art virtual reality technology, the Swappo app provides a dynamic platform enabling individuals to acquire new abilities at no expense of any educational fees. This approach enhances accessibility and economy in learning. The platform incorporates features like instant feedback provision, algorithms that match skills with appropriate tasks, and versatile interactive tools customized for varying proficiencies. Consequently, the experience is informative, productive & satisfying while managing an individual's valuable time investment in effective learning methods. By democratizing access to an array of educational opportunities, this approach fosters continuous learning and collaboration in the digital era. This sets a foundation for transformative movements towards sharing skills and personal growth.

The Clutterization problem

In today's fast-paced and consumer-driven society, individuals find themselves grappling with an increasing number of possessions, leading to overwhelming clutter and a sense of being weighed down by belongings.

With the advent of ever-growing online marketplaces globally, it has become easier than ever to buy and sell used products. However, a glaring gap remains: the lack of a dedicated platform for bartering and swapping goods and services. Traditional flea markets provide a nostalgic experience but often have limited product offerings and are predominantly one-way transactions—either selling or buying, with little room for bartering.

This absence of a comprehensive and efficient digital platform for swapping and bartering presents significant problems for users. Many individuals yearn for a more sustainable and cost-effective way to obtain new items while simultaneously reducing waste and de-cluttering their homes. They desire a platform that encourages meaningful exchanges, fosters a sense of community, and offers a diverse range of products and services available for bartering.

Furthermore, people often struggle with the asymmetry of their needs and wants. They may have a particular item they wish to part with, but finding someone willing to swap that item for something they desire can be daunting. The absence of an intelligent matching system makes it difficult to find suitable bartering opportunities that align with their budget and preferences.

The challenges users face in bartering and swapping underscore the need for a specialized online platform like Swappo. The app aims to bridge this gap by providing a seamless and efficient solution that not only connects individuals for bartering but also alleviates the burden of excess possessions and fosters a more sustainable approach to consumption.

The VR skill exchange model presents several distinctive challenges beyond those found in conventional product exchanges. Verifying the proficiency and aptitude of participants can prove to be challenging, leading to potential mismatches and dissatisfaction as maintaining quality control becomes more difficult. As there are currently no established industry standards for verifying skills, trust issues may arise that further hinder user engagement in such transactions.

Moreover, the technological constraints of utilizing a VR platform can make certain users hesitate due to the requirement of complex machinery and specific technical knowledge. Additionally, organizing real-time interactions between individuals in various time zones and with different personal schedules presents an obstacle that complicates facilitating skill-sharing efficiently. Consequently, developing solutions to these challenges is essential when creating a functional and inclusive VR Barter System designed to improve Swappo's overall user experience.

In the upcoming sections, we will explore how Swappo addresses these pain points by offering a user-friendly platform that matches individuals based on their desired exchanges, budgetary constraints, and preferences. By bringing together like-minded individuals and enabling them to connect, Swappo revolutionizes the way we think about goods and services exchange within our communities.

Execution Strategies

The successful implementation of Swappo relies on effective execution strategies which ensure a seamless and user-friendly experience for its users. By inculcating various methodologies, Swappo maximizes its potential to revolutionize goods and services exchange within the community.

User Interface and Flow: The user interface and flow of the Swappo app play a crucial role in providing a streamlined experience. Upon registration, users are prompted to input their location, select relevant product/service categories, and provide detailed descriptions accompanied by photos. This information forms the foundation for Swappo's intelligent matching system.

Simultaneous Publishing of Requests: To facilitate efficient exchanges, Swappo employs simultaneous publishing of the exchange requests. This approach ensures that requests to sell a particular item are published only when corresponding requests to buy the same or similar item are also present. By synchronizing these requests, Swappo establishes a fair and balanced platform for bartering, promoting meaningful exchanges that meet the needs and desires of both parties involved.

Advanced AI Algorithms: To enhance the user experience, Swappo utilizes advanced AI algorithms. These algorithms analyze user preferences, budgetary constraints, and the selected product/service categories to deliver tailored recommendations. By leveraging AI, Swappo narrows down the vast array of listings and presents users with a curated list of potential swap options, enabling them to explore suitable exchanges effortlessly.

User Feedback and Ratings: Swappo emphasizes the importance of user feedback and ratings to maintain a reliable and trustworthy community. Users are encouraged to provide feedback on their bartering experiences, allowing others to make informed decisions based on the reputation and reliability of their potential swap partners.

Robust VR Platform: A careful strategy must be followed to effectively execute the Virtual Reality (VR) Barter System, so that participants may enjoy a seamless and captivating experience. The initial steps entail constructing an impressive VR platform that incorporates sophisticated algorithms for skill-matching along with immersive virtual settings specific to various skills, for instance, culinary demonstrations or pottery workshops taking place in a virtual kitchen or pottery studio respectively.

Integration of User Feedback and Interaction: To ensure an effective exchange of skills and dynamic learning, the platform should enable users to be able to interact in real time and provide feedback. It is crucial to continually update the system based on user feedback to maintain its relevance while enhancing the overall user experience.

Verification Process: One way to resolve proficiency problems in the VR Barter System is by introducing a system for verifying users' skills, which can enhance their credibility. Different categories could include asking individuals to provide relevant documents including certifications, participate in skill evaluations or gain endorsements from peers. Besides that, integrating feedback and rating mechanisms enables participants to evaluate each other's abilities better while also cultivating trust within the community. Social media integration within the profile of the users can help in verifying credentials. This feature will be available exclusively to the paid users and not to the freemium version.

Scheduling Tools: To address the issue of different time zones, the platform will incorporate scheduling options that take into account various regions/time zones. This will enable users to discover a common schedule for exchanging skills. To reduce conflicts due to time constraints, an alternative learning method could be to provide self-paced tutorials and recorded sessions which would enable the participants to access skill sharing opportunities at their convenience would make it possible for participants to access skill-sharing opportunities at their convenience.

Building a community: To ensure the VR Barter System's success as an innovative skill exchange platform, it is crucial to create a robust and lively community via focused outreach efforts and collaborations with current networks that promote mutual knowledge sharing. Enabling users by providing in-depth support such as tutorials and customer service is vital for maximizing their participation while bolstering engagement.

Throughout its execution, Swappo prioritizes user satisfaction, ease of use, and security. By adopting these implementation methodologies, Swappo ensures that the platform offers a seamless and efficient environment for individuals to connect, barter, and engage in mutually beneficial exchanges.

Further, we will explore the revenue models employed by Swappo to sustain its operations, as well as the social impact it can create by providing a platform for responsible disposal and gifting to NGOs.

Revenue Models for Sustainable Operations

For Swappo to operate sustainably and continue providing its valuable services, it employs a combination of revenue models that ensure financial viability while offering added benefits to its users.

Commission on Successful Transactions: One of the primary revenue streams for Swappo is a small commission charged for facilitating successful transactions and providing escrow services. This commission-based approach ensures that Swappo can cover its operational costs while offering a secure platform for users to engage in bartering and swapping with peace of mind.

Logistics Services: Swappo capitalizes on the logistics involved in the pick-up and drop-off services. Users who prefer the convenience of having their items delivered to their doorstep can also opt for Swappo's logistics service, generating revenue from the associated delivery fees. This not only enhances the user experience but also provides an additional avenue of revenue generation.

Partnerships with Recyclers and NGOs: Beyond facilitating transactions, Swappo acknowledges the significance of social impact. Therefore, the platform collaborates with NGOs and authorized recyclers, establishing a revenue-sharing model. When users choose to gift their items to NGOs through Swappo, a portion of the revenue generated from subsequent sales or utilization of those items is shared with the partnering NGOs. Similarly, authorized recyclers receive a portion of the revenue generated from recycling or repurposing items, promoting environmental sustainability.

Subscription and In-platform Purchases: By adopting a subscription model, the VR Barter System will levy users with either monthly or annual charges to avail premium features like exclusive environments, advanced skill-matching and priority support. This would ensure a steady income for the system consistently. Moreover, it will also gain revenue through transaction fees on in-platform purchases as well as usage of exceptional services such as virtual tools and materials.

Partnership with Institutions and Workshops: Collaborations with academic institutions and commercial entities to host online workshops and promotions can provide an additional source of revenue. This method of obtaining income diversifies our financial strategy, strengthens user engagement, and encourages the sharing of expertise.

By diversifying its revenue streams, Swappo ensures a stable financial model that aligns with its core values of promoting sustainability and social impact. These revenue models not only support Swappo's operations but also contribute to the well-being of the community and the environment.

In the subsequent section, we will examine how Swappo can facilitate the redistribution of items to those in need through NGOs and promote responsible disposal through authorized recyclers.

Social Impact: Promoting Sustainability and Community Support

Swappo holds tremendous potential to create a positive social impact when made available to the masses. By providing a dedicated platform for bartering and swapping goods and services, Swappo encourages sustainable consumption practices and significantly reduces waste.

Redistribution of Items: One significant social impact of Swappo is the redistribution of items in a decent condition to those in need. Through partnerships with NGOs, Swappo facilitates the gifting of items to individuals and communities who can benefit from them. This not only helps address the needs of less fortunate individuals but also promotes a sense of community support and solidarity.

Global Inclusivity and Collaboration: The VR Barter System advocates for a worldwide exchange of expertise, nurturing an inclusive and cooperative environment for education. Through its easily accessible platform that facilitates knowledge-sharing beyond borders, it equips individuals with cost-effective means to acquire skills over time. This model not only bolsters communal bonds but also supports environmental protection by lessening the demand for physical resources and travel required in conventional learning methodologies.

Environmental Sustainability: Swappo takes environmental sustainability seriously by promoting responsible disposal of items through authorized recyclers. Items that are no longer usable or in poor condition can be recycled or repurposed into new products, reducing the strain on landfills and minimizing environmental impact.

By fostering a culture of reusing and repurposing, Swappo encourages users to adopt more sustainable consumption habits. It promotes a shift away from the "throwaway" culture and encourages individuals to value and extend the lifespan of their possessions.

Conclusion

Swappo represents an innovative and transformative solution for the exchange of goods and services within communities. By embracing the bartering system, Swappo fosters a sense of community, promotes sustainability, and empowers individuals to de-clutter their lives while acquiring desired items in a cost-effective manner.

Swappo Revolution- Value Meets Opportunity

Chapter- 4

Celeb Connect: Learn with Stars

"Celeb Connect: Learn with Stars" is not just a name but it reflects the fundamental purpose of the platform. The idea behind this title stemmed from an earnest desire among the thinkers to bring famous personalities (celebrities) and their followers closer together, allowing individuals access to top-notch guidance and education.

In the vibrant tapestry of India, a strong urge for self-improvement and education resonates among individuals who idolize celebrities and influencers. Whether in sports, academics, dance, digital marketing, communication skills or counselling, aspiring learners encounter various obstacles. High costs of learning from their role models, coupled with limited accessibility attributed to geographic barriers make such mentorship seem unattainable.

Riya, a tech visionary with an entrepreneurial spirit, identified an unmet need through extensive market research. Her team's thorough analysis revealed that there was a remarkable 68% surge in online searches for coaching programs led by celebrities over the past year. Furthermore, their survey results indicated that as many as 82% of respondents expressed keen interest in participating if these programs became more accessible - signifying significant potential and opportunity.

Launching Celeb Connect

Riya used these insights to launch Celeb Connect, an innovative platform aimed at democratizing learning via technology. The user-friendly interface served as a virtual meeting point that connected individuals from diverse communities around India with their favorite celebrities for educational purposes and eliminated traditional access barriers in the process.

What set Celeb Connect apart was its distinctive value proposition. Users could recommend their desired celebrity mentors, outline preferred coursework arrangements, and suggest reasonable fees, Celeb Connect set itself apart with a distinctive value proposition. This collaborative approach struck a chord with the audience as it encouraged them to take ownership of their learning endeavors.

Take Rahul, an aspiring cricketer from Mumbai who yearned for the mentorship of a former cricketing legend. Similarly, Priya, a communications enthusiast in Delhi wanted to refine her skills under a renowned public speaker. They both met at Celeb Connect where they bonded with communities that shared their zeal to learn and gain insights from their idols.

With strong market intelligence driving its operations, Celeb Connect was able to draw in a broad spectrum of stars spanning Bollywood, sports, education and marketing as well as motivational speaking. The platform's capacity to enhance an influencer's audience extent through collaborative coaching sessions by 43% proved irresistible for many celebrities who viewed it as the perfect chance to interact with fans directly while streamlining their interactions.

Building a Learning Hub

Many celebrities were enthusiastic about strengthening their bonds with fans and promoting accessible learning, leading them to sign up for sessions on Celeb Connect. Eventually, this platform transformed into an interactive centre where individuals from different backgrounds came together to exchange ideas, gain new perspectives and improve themselves through the guidance of their role models. This exemplified a commitment towards data-driven creativity as well as the collective pursuit of knowledge.

Riya utilized market insights and compelling data by incorporating technology, resulting in the creation of Celeb Connect. This app served as a means of connection and a catalyst for accessible learning opportunities throughout India. By highlighting its ability to transform through the use of data-driven solutions showcased how transformative power was attainable through this platform.

Market Analysis Insights for Celeb Connect

Demographic Analysis

- **Age Groups**: Among the 18-25 age group, 60% expressed interest in sports coaching while 40% favored personal development courses.

- **Locations:** Bollywood actors and digital influencers sparked substantial interest, particularly in tier-2 and tier-3 cities where 55% of users were captivated by these personalities.

- **Professions/Education Levels:** IT professionals notably favored digital marketing courses (40%), highlighting a demand for industry-specific learning.

Demand Analysis

- Search Trends: The demand for coaching programs saw a significant rise during major sporting events, movie releases, and influencer campaigns. This highlights the strong connection between entertainment events and interest in such programs.

Social Media Engagement: Twitter and Instagram emerged as key platforms, with video content generating 25% more engagement than static posts or text-based content

Competitor Analysis:

- **Existing Platforms:** Despite having smaller user bases than their competitors, Celeb Connect distinguished itself by providing unparalleled access to high-profile celebrities.

Users favored platforms that provided rare opportunities for exclusive interactions with the most influential personalities in various industries.

- **Strengths and Weaknesses:** Pricing structures were cited as a major pain point, with users seeking more flexible payment options or bundled packages for multiple courses.

User Preferences:

- **Preferred Celebrities/Influencers:** Within the digital influencer category, makeup and lifestyle influencers accounted for 60% of preferences, indicating a strong interest in lifestyle and beauty-related coaching.

- **Preferred Learning Formats:** Among the demographic aged 26-35, majority (70%) preferred entirely virtual sessions due to work-related time constraints.

- **Pricing Sensitivity:** Respondents indicated willingness to pay a premium (up to INR 8000) for intensive, hands-on workshops spanning multiple sessions with industry experts.

Feasibility and Scalability:

- **Technical Infrastructure:** The platform's scalable infrastructure extends beyond user capacity to incorporate AI-driven recommendation engines for personalized course suggestions and content curation.

- **Partnership Opportunities:** Collaboration negotiations with celebrities focus on co-branding initiatives and interactive engagement beyond course sessions, aiming to enhance user loyalty and engagement.

Financial Projections:

Market Size Projection: Emerging data suggests a steady 15% annual growth in the celebrity-led coaching industry, projecting a market size of INR 600 million by the end of the next fiscal year.

Survey and Feedback:

- **Feedback Insights:** Respondents emphasized the need for post-course engagement and continued mentorship, indicating a potential market for alumni programs or extended coaching subscriptions.

- **Regional Preferences:** Southern regions of India showed a higher inclination towards dance and art-related coaching, signaling the need for region-specific content and celebrity collaborations.

Celeb Connect Benefits and Features

Celeb Connect revolutionizes the learning process, going beyond conventional transactional methods. Boasting a wide range of programs and an expansive outlook on education, this platform is committed to delivering tailored, engaging lessons that revamp traditional learning paradigms for all learners.

Secure Transactions

Celeb Connect ensures secure financial transactions by serving as an intermediary between users and celebrity coaches. By using strong encryption protocols and payment gateways, it assures that the customers' financial information remains safe and confidential, instilling confidence among its user base.

Personalized Course Recommendations

Celeb Connect employs advanced algorithms and machine learning techniques to examine user activities and interests, in order to provide customized course options. Analyzing the behavior of users as well as their historical patterns facilitates Celeb Connect in recommending tailored courses that optimize harmonious connections between users and courses.

Vibrant Community Engagement

Celeb Connect fosters a dynamic and interactive community within its platform. It offers users the opportunity to engage in discussions, share insights, seek advice from coaches, collaborate through forums, and do live Q&A sessions, and chat groups. The platform also incorporates gamification elements like achievement badges and progress trackers, encouraging active participation and fostering a sense of accomplishment among users.

Comprehensive Learning Experience

Beyond transactional facilitation, the platform ensures a rich and comprehensive learning experience. It goes the extra mile by curating diverse course offerings, scouting industry-relevant courses led by eminent influencers, and subjecting them to a rigorous vetting process.   This ensures that users have access to high-quality content that meets their learning objectives.

Feedback Mechanisms and Continuous Improvement

Celeb Connect prioritizes user feedback and employs robust mechanisms to gather insights on-course experiences, coach effectiveness, and platform usability. Through sentiment analysis and data-driven feedback, it continuously refines its offerings to enhance course quality and user experience. This iterative approach ensures that the platform evolves in line with user preferences and industry trends.

Facilitating Engagement Beyond Courses

Recognizing the need for ongoing engagement and mentorship, Celeb Connect is exploring avenues for post-course interaction. It aims to create alumni programs or extended coaching subscriptions that enable users to maintain connections with coaches and peers even after completing a course.

Advanced AI Features

Celeb Connect incorporates state-of-the-art AI technology to enhance the learning experience and facilitate significant interactions between users and celebrities. With its AI-powered features, the platform transforms how individuals engage with, discover, and gain knowledge from their preferred role models across various domains.

Personalized Learning

The process of AI integration on Celeb Connect commences by comprehending the unique preferences, learning history, and aspirations of each user. Through analyzing their patterns of engagement and behavior, it then identifies personalized pathways for growth that align with individual interests. With an array of ambitions whether users who want to learn how to play guitar or users who want to learn cricket from their favorite player or a user who wants to learn the specifics of how to fly a drone, a user who wants to learn theatre from a favorite celebrity or an influencer, AI recommends a set list of suitable celebrity coaches who offer tailored courses designed to meet users' needs.

Smart Group Formation

Utilizing artificial intelligence, users are grouped into cohesive learning communities founded on their common interests and objectives. This characteristic enables the establishment of distinct groups centered around particular niches such as guitar enthusiasts, cricket aficionados, drone technology explorers or aspiring actors. Through uniting individuals with comparable passions under a shared banner AI cultivates an environment that is supportive where members can collaborate harmoniously to exchange insights and grow collectively while benefiting from the guidance provided by well-known influencers.

USP: Dynamic Matchmaking

The heart of Celeb Connect's AI capabilities lies in its capacity to pair users with appropriate celebrity trainers and influencers. By analyzing the user's preferences, course requirements, and budget limitations, the AI suggests ideal matches between celebrities and their followers.

Additionally, users can create customized courses that include specific participant numbers or desired pricing expectations prompting the system to arrange transparent negotiations for both parties involved. This feature ensures a mutually beneficial arrangement taking into consideration alignment with expected standards while considering availability from celebs' end as well by ultimately delivering effective engagements suited for all concerned individuals involved seamlessly through our platform!

Automated Negotiations

The use of AI technology in the negotiation process helps to simplify it by automating price modifications and aiding transparent communication between users and celebrities. Celeb Connect utilizes advanced algorithms powered with artificial intelligence, enabling real-time negotiations wherein either party can propose changes concerning quoted fees or terms during the discussion. This feature encourages equitable pricing techniques while enhancing user satisfaction through its flexible engagement policies that offer transparency at all times.

Celeb Connect's AI solution is constantly adapting and improving. Through the use of predictive recommendation engines, it has become adept at anticipating user preferences and making personalized course suggestions. This is achieved through machine learning algorithms that can detect popular topics, and emerging trends in various industries, ultimately enriching each learner's experience with relevant insights tailored to their evolving interests or career goals. With this proactive approach to learning content recommendations, users receive timely advice aligned perfectly for them as they embark towards achieving their aspirations!

Enhanced Community Engagement

The AI on Celeb Connect goes beyond mere matchmaking and recommendations. It boasts interactive features that personalize engagements to enhance user experience, such as hosting live Q&A sessions, exclusive webinars, and virtual meet-and-greet opportunities with celebrities—facilitated by seamless scheduling and participation thanks to the platform's cutting-edge technology. These experiences aim at deepening relationships between users and influencers whilst fostering ongoing mentorship programs for knowledge-sharing purposes.

Continuous Improvements

Celeb Connect continues to prioritize AI innovation as it grows, working towards ongoing improvements and enhancements that put users first. Upcoming advancements will further utilize AI capabilities to optimize course delivery methods, refine feedback channels, and introduce advanced analytics for tracking performance outcomes and learning progress. By embracing the potential of cutting-edge technology-driven solutions within education paradigms today, Celeb Connect is able to offer its users unparalleled access to celebrity mentorship while revolutionizing traditional approaches towards skill-building success.

Strategic Marketing and Partnerships

Celeb Connect pursues strategic collaborations with educational institutions, industry leaders, and influencers to expand the platform's course offerings, boost credibility within specific domains, and increase its visibility through targeted marketing initiatives. These efforts keep Celeb Connect at the forefront of delivering personalized and high-quality learning experiences.

Direct Engagement with Celebrities

This innovative platform allows users to engage directly with their admired celebrities, offering personalized mentoring, coaching, and guidance from industry icons across various fields. This pioneering feature enables users to forge personalized connections and gain invaluable insights from their idols.

Motivation and Inspiration

Beyond technical expertise, direct engagement with celebrities serves as a source of motivation and inspiration for users. The personal anecdotes, success stories, and guidance shared by these icons encourage users to pursue their goals and aspirations with renewed vigor.

Personalized Mentorship

Celeb Connect offers a unique opportunity for personalized mentorship directly from industry icons. This goes beyond the conventional learning experience, providing users with tailored advice, expertise, and techniques curated by the celebrities themselves.

Direct Interaction and Q&A Sessions

The Direct Interaction and Q&A Sessions on Celeb Connect create an engaging and immersive learning environment for users to interact with their beloved celebrities. This interactive platform allows users to connect with their idols through various mediums, whether online, physical, or a blend of both, fostering a unique and enriched educational experience.

- **Live Interactions**

Celeb Connect hosts live sessions where users can interact with celebrities in real-time. This format enables immediate interaction, allowing users to ask questions, seek advice, and receive responses directly from their idols. Live interactions facilitate a Sense of immediacy and connection, making the learning experience more dynamic and engaging.

- **Q&A Sessions:**

The platform hosts dedicated Q&A sessions where users can submit questions in advance or in real-time. Celebrities address these questions, offering insights, solutions, and personalized advice. This format encourages an exchange of ideas, enabling users to gain valuable knowledge and guidance directly from industry icons.

- **Exclusive Webinars:**

Celeb Connect offers exclusive webinars with celebrities, diving deep into specific topics for a structured, comprehensive learning experience.

- **Online and Physical Engagement:**

The platform offers flexibility in engagement formats, catering to users' preferences. Users can participate in virtual sessions from anywhere, allowing for widespread accessibility. Additionally, Celeb Connect also endeavors to arrange physical meet-and-greet sessions, workshops, or masterclasses in select locations, providing an unparalleled hands-on learning experience for interested users.

- **Immersive Learning Experience:**

Through these diverse interaction modes, Celeb Connect fosters an immersive and interactive learning environment empowering user to actively engage with their favorite celebrities, seek guidance, and gain valuable insights.

- **Blending Online and Physical Learning:**

Celeb Connect integrates online and physical engagements. This hybrid approach allows users the flexibility to participate based on their preferences and geographical constraints, ensuring an inclusive and accessible learning experience for all.

Conclusion

Celeb Connect emerges as a dynamic, comprehensive learning ecosystem, transcending the educational paradigms. It offers secure, personalized access for users to engage with their cherished celebrity mentors. Through Celeb Connect, users embark on a journey of diverse learning opportunities, each tailored to foster continuous growth within an interactive, ever-evolving learning landscape

Chapter-5

Serenify Pods: Personalized Mental Wellness Pods

Serenify takes after the term "serene," representing a sense of peace and calm, along with "ify" which implies an action or transformation. The brand title embodies the pod's ultimate objective: to transform any space into a sanctuary of tranquility, assisting people in attaining both mental composure and overall well-being.

With the ever-increasing speed and demand of our world, mental well-being is emerging as an urgent concern. The challenges brought forth by modern times can significantly affect our psychological health - be it work-related stress, personal connections or information overload.

However, traditional methods to address these issues like therapy sessions and wellness retreats often require people to commit their time; something that may be hard to find in this busy life we lead today.

Introducing Serenify Pods - an innovative answer that combines technology, ease and mental well-being. These unique pods provide customized mental wellness guidance and are a revolutionary approach towards accessible psychiatric treatment. The sound-insulated capsules incorporate advanced tech features to create havens of peacefulness for stress relief and rejuvenation amid everyday hassles. Strategically stationed in frequently visited locations such as commercial buildings, public parks, airports or shopping centres; they supply quick yet powerful personalized psych services on the move!

Serenify Pods set themselves apart by providing personalized mental health experiences. Their sessions are tailored to suit each user's present state of mind, individual inclinations and objectives through cutting-edge technologies like AI and biometric sensors that ensure real-time adaptation. Such a customized approach guarantees top-notch care for every client; be it brief relief from work-related tension or profound meditative moments.

In addition, Serenify Pods offer an all-encompassing sensory journey that merges sound, sight, and touch to craft a relaxing ambience. The pods come equipped with adjustable lighting options, aromatherapy features as well as temperature controls, elevating relaxation to the next level by ensuring every session is a complete wellness adventure.

Although the benefits of using these pods are evident, there are multiple difficulties associated with their implementation such as high initial expenses, upkeep troubles and possible privacy concerns. To conquer these hindrances, careful planning is necessary along with strong data security protocols and instructive user training.

Serenify Pods aim to revolutionize the mental wellness industry by incorporating partnerships, diverse monetization tactics and a strong dedication towards data privacy within their transparent operational model. Through discreet, personalized access to mental health support services, Serenify Pods could potentially pave the way for healthier individuals and communities in the future.

We will examine the concept and possibilities of Serenify Pods by taking a closer look at their structure, distinct features that make them stand out in the market, operating mechanisms as well as tackling some challenges they hope to solve. This groundbreaking method towards mental well-being offers the potential for remarkable growth in individual and organizational wellness while possibly establishing new benchmarks for brain-care practices in our community.

Insights on Market Analysis for Serenify Pods

1. **Demographic Analysis**
   - **Target Audience:** Serenify Pods are tailored to meet the needs of a wide spectrum of users, as mental wellness solutions are becoming increasingly necessary. The main demographic includes:
   - **Working Professionals:** Working professionals, especially those in high-pressure fields like finance, technology, and healthcare industries frequently requiring swift and efficient stress-reduction choices.

- **Frequent Travelers:** Individuals who travel often, such as professionals on business trips or vacationers passing through airports and transit terminals, can derive advantages from relaxation techniques and mental wellness amenities during layovers or before extended flights.

- **Urban Residents:** People living in urban areas experience stress regularly due to the demands of city life and may not have convenient access to conventional healthcare services.

- **Students:** College and university students facing academic stress who require frequent mental refreshment breaks.

- **Elderly Individuals:** Those in their advanced years who could avail themselves of serene and calming environments that promote emotional wellness.

- **Age:** The pods are intended for all to use but cater primarily to working-age adults and students, with the age range estimated between 18-65.

2. **Demand Analysis**

The Increasing Recognition of Mental Health:

- The significance of mental health is becoming more acknowledged, as an increasing number of individuals are opting for means to cope with stress and enhance their overall state. This tendency has been reinforced by wider media attention and discussions concerning psychological well-being in society.

Demand for Convenience:

- The demand for easily accessible mental wellness options is propelled by the contemporary, fast-paced lifestyle. To meet this need, Serenify Pods offer a portable and convenient solution ideal for those on the go.

Corporate Wellness:

- To enhance productivity and minimize absenteeism, companies are progressively allocating funds towards staff wellness schemes. Serenify Pods present a worthwhile augmentation to such programs.

Impact of the COVID-19 Pandemic:

Due to the COVID-19 pandemic, people's attention towards mental health problems has increased. Consequently, there is a surge in demand for easily available wellness services that offer a feeling of security and confidentiality.

3. **Competitor Analysis**

    - **Meditation Apps**: Serenify Pods offer a more immersive and multi-sensory experience in comparison to the digital, on-demand mental wellness solutions provided by Meditation Apps despite their convenience.

    - **Wellness and Therapy Centres**: Serenify Pods offer quick and accessible sessions while Therapy and Wellness Centres provide in-depth mental health support that requires more time and commitment.

- **Spa and Wellness Retreats**: They offer immersive relaxation but may not be easily accessible for frequent indulgence.

The Competitive Advantage:

- It can be personalized and tailored to fit individual needs using biometric data as well as AI.
- Conveniently located in areas of high traffic, with no requirement for prior scheduling.
- Incorporation of cutting-edge functionalities such as ambient sound, aroma therapy, guided meditation and therapeutic lighting, all of this while relaxing on a massage chair.
- Offers a private and serene environment to support mental well-being.

4. Feasibility and Scalability

Feasibility:

- Serenify Pods can be easily equipped with the necessary technology, including AI, biometric sensors and soundproofing, as these components are readily available for integration.
- It is operationally feasible to manage the pods through a blend of remote monitoring and periodic on-site maintenance. They are easily installable in high-traffic areas with little disturbance.

Scalability:

- Serenify Pods have the potential for market expansion as they can be utilized in various regions and tailored to suit local preferences and requirements.

- Collaborating with corporations, public institutions, and wellness centres creates partnership opportunities that enable quick scaling and integration of services into already established wellness programs.
- Several revenue streams, such as pay-per-use, subscriptions, and corporate partnerships, enable scalability and financial sustainability for our business.

Challenges:

- **Initial Costs**: The upfront expenses include significant investments in technology, installation and marketing. Nonetheless, cost reduction can be achieved through economies of scale once it achieves market traction.
- **Maintenance**: Efficient management of regular maintenance, ensuring cleanliness and functionality can be ensured with the help of a dedicated support team.

5. **Survey and Feedback:**

- **Interest in Pods**: According to surveys, there is a great deal of interest in mental wellness solutions that can be accessed on demand, with working professionals and frequent travelers showing a very high level of enthusiasm.
- **Interest in Features**: Features that are highly favored by users include guided meditation, customizable environments, and data privacy.

- **Sensitivity for Pricing**: When it comes to mental wellness services, users are willing to pay. However, they tend to favor pricing models that provide flexibility and good value for their money.

Continuous Improvements:

- To refine and enhance the features and services of pods, user feedback is regularly collected and analyzed in a loop.

- To keep the pods relevant and attractive, it is vital to stay abreast of the latest trends in both mental wellness and technology. Therefore, adaptation to these evolving developments becomes imperative.

6. Financial Projections

- The Subscription Model is expected to produce a consistent revenue stream while also having the potential for annual growth of 20% and a market size of ₹300 million due to an increasing number of users choosing ongoing availability.

- The Pay-Per-Use model is predicted to generate substantial earnings, particularly from densely populated areas. Projections indicate that utilization rates are expected to grow by 15% annually.

- Anticipated to drive significant revenue, Corporate Partnerships offer a reliable and substantial income stream through the purchase of bulk packages and wellness offerings.

Timeline for Profitability:

- The Break-Even Point is anticipated to be achieved in the next 2 to 3 years, despite the significant initial investment expenses that will be balanced out by increasing revenue sources.

- Over the next five years, sustainable profitability and a noteworthy expansion of market share are expected to be realized for long-term growth.

The Market Potential:

- With a high demand for mental wellness solutions in international markets, there is an opportunity for global expansion, leading to a further revenue boost.

Serenify Pods present a hopeful answer for easily accessible and tailored mental well-being, as proven through careful market analysis and foresightful preparation. These groundbreaking pods possess the capacity to profoundly influence the realm of mental wellness by offering simple yet efficient assistance to individuals from diverse demographics. The insights gathered here establish a solid framework for entering the market successfully with continued expansion, positioning Serenify Pods at the forefront of advancing future solutions in this field.

Operating Model for Serenify Pods

Serenify Pods will be placed in high-traffic and high-stress areas to guarantee optimum accessibility and visibility. By collaborating with various organizations such as corporations, airports, shopping malls and public institutions, Serenify aims to locate the pods at places where people often look for opportunities for relaxation and mental wellness. These partnerships would help set up the installations effectively.

- **Corporate Offices**: Collaborate with corporations to establish pods inside offices, enabling workers easy access to mental wellness breaks amidst their work hours.

- **Airports**: To assist travelers in dealing with flying-related stress and anxiety, it is recommended to install pods at departure lounges and waiting areas of airports.

- **Shopping centres**: Introduce pods within its premises where visitors can seek refuge from the hustle and bustle while indulging in a rejuvenating experience.

- **Public Institutions**: Collaborate with public libraries, government facilities, and universities to provide mental health services that reach a wider range of people.

- **Mental Health Professionals:** Partner with renowned therapists and psychiatrists to integrate Serenify Pods into their therapy or counseling sessions, as a supplementary tool for relaxation, mindfulness, and stress reduction.

Through a mobile app, individuals have the option to reserve sessions and receive information regarding pod availability, session types, as well as pricing. In addition to this feature, there are kiosks nearby each pod that provide an alternative booking method for expedited and effortless access.

Monetization Strategy:

Serenify Pods plans to generate revenue from various sources through a multi-faceted monetization approach that caters to the diverse needs and preferences of its users.

- **Subscription Model**: The Subscription Model allows users to opt for either a monthly or annual plan enabling them to avail of unlimited access to the pods at discounted rates. This model incentivizes frequent usage and ensures regular revenue flow.

- **Pay-per-use**: If flexibility is what you seek, then our Pay-Per-Use alternative might suit your needs. You can choose to pay for each session individually, and the pricing will vary depending on the length of time and type of session selected.

- **Corporate Partnership**: Tailored packages are available for corporations interested in incorporating Serenify Pods into their employee wellness initiatives. Options include purchasing sessions in bulk or creating personalized subscription plans.

- **Sponsorships and Ads**: Partner with wellness brands to sponsor pods and display non-intrusive ads during sessions or provide product samples, creating an extra revenue stream while adding value for users through relevant wellness content.

Session Management:

Serenify Pods' value proposition is based on customized session management that employs artificial intelligence to cater to each user's specific requirements for an optimal mental well-being experience.

- **The Guided Programs**: Users have the option to select from a diverse range of guided programs that are customized to suit their requirements, such as mindfulness exercises for relaxation, methods aimed at reducing stress levels, techniques designed for augmenting energy levels and strategies developed specifically to improve concentration.

- **AI-Powered Customization**: Through AI-Powered Customization, the pods' advanced system will evaluate feedback from users and examine biometric indicators such as heart rate and stress levels to adapt to the environment in real time. This approach guarantees that every session is optimally tailored to each user's current mental state, resulting in a one-of-a-kind and efficient experience with each use.

Support and Maintenance:

Maintaining the good condition of Serenify Pods is essential to preserve user satisfaction and operational efficiency.

- **Frequent Maintenance Checks**: Scheduled maintenance checks will be carried out to guarantee the smooth and dependable operation of all equipment, particularly pods.

- **Hygiene Protocol**: To uphold a clean and inviting atmosphere, hygiene protocols will entail routine cleaning services. Given the current emphasis on health precautions in light of the pandemic, proactive hygiene measures are crucial.

- **Customer Support**: Users can seek assistance for any technical or user issues through the mobile app or a specialized hotline provided by customer support. This ensures efficient problem-solving and boosts user satisfaction with the experience as a whole.

Data Privacy and Security:

Strict protocols will be followed by Serenify Pods to safeguard user information, emphasizing the significance of data privacy and security.

- **Compliance with Privacy Regulations**: The system guarantees adherence to data privacy regulations, keeping users' information collected, stored and processed securely.

- **Encryption and Anonymization of Data**: To prevent unauthorized access, all user data will undergo encryption. Additionally, personal information shall be anonymized to guarantee the confidentiality of identities and ensure privacy protection.

- **Communication and Transparency**: Users will receive clear information about the collected data types, their intended use, and rights over their personal information. This transparent approach fosters trust and reassures users that their privacy is respected.

User Education and Marketing:

For driving adoption and creating awareness about the benefits of Serenify Pods, essential elements are efficient marketing strategies and educating users.

- **Social Media Campaigns and Influencers**: To broaden the reach, use social media channels and partner with mental health influencers and advocates for Serenify Pods. The campaign will emphasize its distinctive qualities to persuade potential users to experience it firsthand.

- **Introductory Offers or Free Trials**: Provide free trials and introductory sessions to entice fresh users, enabling them to directly experience the advantages. By doing so, any initial reluctance can be overcome while fostering a user community through favorable encounters and referrals.

Serenify Pods strives to cultivate a mental health-aware culture in diverse environments by offering personalized and easily accessible support through its extensive operational framework. This approach aims to cater to the needs of a vast range of users seeking mental wellness assistance.

The AI-Powered Customization

Using cutting-edge artificial intelligence (AI) algorithms, the Serenify Pods provide customized mental wellness experiences that cater to individual needs and preferences. This personalized approach improves session effectiveness while guaranteeing a user-friendly interface for ultimate convenience.

Serenify Pods' AI customization is built around its capability to study user data in real time. When users step into the pod, they are requested to enter fundamental information regarding their present mental state and choices using an instinctive interface. This primary input is combined with biometric data gathered from integrated sensors (e.g., heart rate monitors and skin conductance sensors), developing a foundation for decision-making facilitated by artificial intelligence.

The AI uses real-time data analysis to choose from a range of guided meditation programs, relaxation techniques and ambient environments. These are specifically targeted towards addressing mental states like stress, anxiety, fatigue or the need for clarity and focus. The AI personalizes each session based on user feedback and physiological responses throughout the experience.

The Serenify Pods elevate the meditation experience by incorporating customizable lighting, immersive soundscapes, and soothing aromatherapy. This multi-sensory approach cultivates a holistic sense of well-being. Additionally, cutting-edge AI technology fine-tunes this sensory integration through real-time biometric data analysis and user feedback to optimize results over time. Serenify Pods become more responsive and effective over time as machine learning algorithms constantly enhance personalized recommendations through user feedback and collected data.

Expanding the Vision: Additional Considerations

Serenify Pods can achieve comprehensive success and make a significant impact on the mental wellness industry by considering various crucial aspects beyond the core operational framework and market projections.

- **Partnerships and Community Engagement**

To improve access to Serenify Pods, collaborating with nearby community centres, schools, and healthcare facilities can be beneficial. This alliance facilitates mental wellness education and amplifies pod utilization amongst various demographic groups. As a result of this unified approach towards supporting mental health awareness, encourages inclusivity.

- **Research and Development (R&D)**

Serenify Pods must maintain their position as a leader in mental wellness technology by consistently investing in research and development. This involves improving AI functionalities, incorporating innovative healing techniques, and responding to evolving user demands with constant feedback analysis.

- **A Global Expansion Strategy**

Although Serenify Pods initially concentrated on domestic markets, formulating a strategic plan for global expansion can enhance their triumph. It's crucial to comprehend the cultural differences, regulatory stipulations and market needs in foreign countries when scaling operations efficiently.

- **Reporting and Impact Measurement**

Incorporating metrics for evaluating the impact of Serenify Pods on users' mental health results is crucial. Collaborating with professionals and researchers in this field can provide significant perspectives on effectiveness, facilitating data-based improvements while establishing measurable advantages for stakeholders.

- **Corporate Social Responsibility Initiatives (CSR)**

The introduction of CSR initiatives can improve Serenify Pods' image and involvement within the community. Such initiatives may include providing reduced-cost sessions for underprivileged groups, backing mental health awareness efforts, or donating a percentage of earnings to organizations that promote research and advocacy towards addressing mental health issues.

- **Modification to Technological Progressions**

By remaining flexible and adept at embracing new technological advancements such as the integration of virtual reality (VR), advanced biometric sensors, or emotion recognition powered by artificial intelligence (AI), Serenify Pods can protect themselves from becoming outdated in the future. Additionally, implementing these technologies will result in increased engagement and satisfaction for users.

- **Mental Health Professionals Collaboration**

By collaborating with licensed therapists and counsellors, Serenify Pods can provide users with access to professional guidance. This enhances their therapeutic benefits and caters to people who have particular mental health requirements.

- **Protocols for Managing a Crisis**

By creating protocols that address emergencies or crises with Serenify Pods, user safety is prioritized and the company's reputation as a trusted mental wellness provider is strengthened. To achieve this, staff members are trained in crisis intervention techniques while also establishing clear communication channels for swift assistance when needed.

AI Customized Solutions

Serenify Pods' main advantage is their utilization of AI in developing personalized wellness experiences. By implementing AI-driven solutions, each session is tailored to address individual user needs, enhancing all aspects of the pod environment based on up-to-date information.

- **Stress Reduction**

Raj, a busy business executive, often feels overwhelmed by the demands of his job. On a particularly stressful day, he steps into a Serenify Pod in his office building. The pod uses AI technology to measure Raj's heart rate and skin conductance as indicators of stress levels before selecting an appropriate guided meditation program that emphasizes deep breathing and mindfulness techniques to help him relax. The pod's illumination switches to a serene blue tone recognized for its calming impact, while the tranquil sounds of lapping waves play gently in the backdrop. Throughout Raj's session, as he progresses further into his journey, AI observes and reacts to his declining heart rate and stress markers by including soothing birdsongs subtly. By the end of it all, Raj feels much calmer and ready to tackle his tasks.

- **Energy Boost**

Let's take another example of a user, Meera. She is a student getting ready for her exams and currently finds herself drained out. She enters the Serenify Pod situated at her university library. The AI inside detects that Meera has a slightly raised heart rate and low skin temperature and chooses an energizing session comprising natural light simulation with refreshing forest sounds to revitalize her spirits quickly. Throughout the session, the AI detects Meera's slightly elevated heart rate indicating revitalized energy levels. To aid in maintaining her concentration, it introduces a mild peppermint aroma recognized for its invigorating properties. Meera leaves the pod feeling rejuvenated and ready to focus on her studies.

- **Focus Enhancement**

As a software developer, Azhar finds it challenging to maintain focus while coding for long hours. He chooses to use his lunch break in the Serenify Pod. By analyzing his data, its AI identifies that although he is calm (as observed by a stable heart rate and even breathing patterns), there's still room for heightened mental awareness in him. It selects an appropriate session that uses soothing binaural beats with rhythmic qualities for stimulating cognitive capabilities thereby increasing focus levels effectively. To enhance concentration, the illumination changes to a pleasant yellow tint while a faint aroma of rosemary scent fills the air which is known for enhancing memory retention. Throughout Azhar's session, the AI scrutinizes his reactions and adjusts conditions accordingly to ensure he remains attentive and engaged. Upon leaving the room, Azhar experiences heightened mental clarity enabling him to tackle complicated tasks with ease.

A Story of Transformation

Anjali, a mother of two, juggling household and work responsibilities, struggles to find any time for self-care and is overwhelmed with stress. While shopping at a mall one day, she stumbled upon Serenify Pod and despite being hesitant about how much some minutes inside the pod could benefit her well-being - decided to try it nonetheless. As soon as Anjali arrived, the touch screen prompted her to provide some essential details about how she was feeling both emotionally and physically.

Based on these inputs, the artificial intelligence detected heightened levels of stress in Anjali's system and automatically selected a session that concentrated on calming her down and alleviating her anxiety. As

Anjali settled into the pod's cozy atmosphere, serene lighting surrounded her while natural sounds from a tropical forest played in tandem with soothing lavender aromas filling up every corner of the space. It had been several months since she felt such immense peace!

Exiting the pod, Anjali experienced a sensation of relief as if an immense burden had been lifted from her shoulders. The brief session granted her the break she craved and provided space for renewed energy while returning to everyday life. Serenify Pods became part of Anjali's routine, offering serenity during valuable moments.

Another example involves a company that installed numerous Serenify Pods in their workplace to promote employee well-being. At first, staffers were hesitant about using the pods as they weren't certain whether utilizing them could truly make an impact on their busy work schedules. However, Rohan, a customer service representative, shared his experience of reduced stress and improved performance after using the pod.

Other employees were inspired by his positive experience with the pods, resulting in an evident enhancement of workplace morale and productivity. The pods swiftly became integral to office culture and contributed towards establishing a less stressful work environment that was more supportive for everyone involved. To summarize, Serenify Pods can strengthen their market position and demonstrate dedication to improving global mental wellness by incorporating these supplementary factors into its core business model. By prioritizing innovation, engaging with the community ethically, implementing ongoing improvements and holding themselves to high standards of excellence; they have a unique opportunity to revolutionize how society views and values mental health for a stronger more resilient future.

Chapter-6

SolarShare: Revolutionizing Energy Access Through Community Sharing

"SolarShare" gets its name from the most efficient method of electricity generation that is, utilizing solar energy and its communal distribution. The term "Solar" denotes eco-friendly, renewable power sourced directly from the sun; whereas "Share," highlights cooperation and sharing among neighbors to allocate surplus solar electricity within a neighborhood that fosters connection for sustainable living.

Introduction

Gazing at the endless expanse of the Texan sky, I felt a pang of frustration. Here we were, bathed in eternal sunshine most days of the year, yet a significant portion of the community struggled with high electricity bills. It was then, during one particularly scorching summer, that the seed of SolarShare was planted. I envisioned a future where communities, and not just corporations, could harness the power of the sun, not just for their own needs, but to also share its bounty with their neighbors. This wasn't just about cost savings; it was about building a more resilient, sustainable, and an interconnected future. However, I knew certain regulations related to the government departments and the ministry of power would need to be carefully navigated and adhered to as per the country's regulations.

Market Research: A Landscape Ripe for Disruption

The sun, constant in our sky, beams down with the promise of altering our energy landscape. Yet, a glaring disparity exists – even being massive, and a free resource, it frequently appears monetarily out of reach. Here's where the tale gets interesting.

Explosive Growth, Stubborn Hurdle

Global Solar Energy Market size was valued at USD 180.78 billion in 2022 and is poised to grow from USD 193.62 billion in 2023 to USD 335.16 billion by 2031, at a CAGR of 7.1% during the forecast period (2024-2031) (Source: SkyQuest Technology report). This demonstrates the growing need for sustainable and renewable energy sources. However, one enduring obstacle is the initial expense of installing solar panels.

Millions in the Dark

While more than 2 million houses in the US have switched to solar power, millions more struggle with the harsh reality of high electricity costs and long for a long-term fix. They recognize the opportunity and the brightness, but the initial outlay serves as a significant barrier.

The Crux of the Challenge

The main obstacle is the cost of installing solar panels on an individual basis. It's a huge shift that makes solar energy unaffordable for many. SolarShare along with other cutting-edge technologies strive to close this gap and maximize the potential of sunshine for everybody.

Beyond Individualism: A Vision for Shared Power

Large-scale solar farms or standalone rooftop installations are the two main choices available to consumers in the conventional solar energy sector. These methods are useful, but they don't solve the issue of cost for a sizable segment of the populace. SolarShare sees an alternative future:

Community Power, Not Individual Burden: Imagine a day in the future when whole communities – rather than just businesses—can harness the power of the sun. Through the promotion of a peer-to-peer energy-sharing network within communities, SolarShare upends the conventional paradigm. The community solar method is an inventive strategy that directly addresses the issue of cost.

Strength in Numbers: Communities that band together can split the upfront costs of installing solar panels. This way, individual homes may profit from solar energy without having to make a large initial investment. SolarShare facilitates this group approach, which benefits the environment as well as individual wallets.

The Need for Disruption is Clear: The results of the market study clearly show that although there is a large affordability barrier, there is still a great demand for solar energy. With its emphasis on community solar sharing networks, SolarShare provides a novel approach that could help realize solar power's full potential. It's a victory for each of us—the individuals, the environment, and the idea of together creating a more sustainable future.

Soaring Costs, Limited Options? SolarShare Offers a Brighter Path

The rising cost of electricity can leave a dent in anyone's wallet, but more so of those struggling financially. On top of that, traditional solar panel systems often come with a hefty upfront price tag and require suitable roof space, further limiting accessibility.

SolarShare is here to change that. We believe everyone deserves access to clean, affordable energy, regardless of their income or roof limitations. That's why we've developed a revolutionary community-based solar energy sharing platform.

Here's how SolarShare tackles the challenges that have kept people in the dark:

- **Slashing Electricity Bills:** SolarShare offers a path to significant cost savings. By subscribing to our community solar garden model, you tap into clean, renewable energy generated by a large solar panel array. This reduces your reliance on traditional, often expensive, energy sources.

- **No Upfront Investment, Just Savings:** Forget the hefty upfront cost! SolarShare eliminates this barrier. You subscribe to our service for a monthly fee, similar to a traditional utility bill. This makes solar energy accessible to everyone, regardless of financial limitations.

- **Roof Space No Longer a Barrier:** SolarShare liberates you from the constraints of your roof. Our community solar gardens are strategically placed, often in partnership with local businesses or landowners with ample space. This eliminates the need for individual rooftop installations, making solar power a viable option for everyone in the community.

By addressing these key pain points, SolarShare empowers you to take control of your energy future and join a movement towards a cleaner, more sustainable world.

SolarShare: Cultivating a Brighter Future, One Community Solar Garden at a Time

Solar Share's cornerstone lies not on individual rooftops but in a network of vibrant **community solar gardens**. Imagine vast fields or rooftops transformed into powerhouses, strategically designed to bathe in sunshine and generate clean energy for your entire neighborhood. These aren't your average backyard setups; they're meticulously planned ecosystems built for shared benefit Let's delve deeper into how these community solar gardens operate:

Partnerships for Progress: SolarShare fosters a collaborative spirit by partnering with local businesses or landowners who possess ample space suitable for large solar panel installations. This could be anything from a decommissioned industrial rooftop to a farmer with a sizable, unused field. These partnerships achieve two key goals: securing ideal locations for the gardens and fostering a sense of community ownership in the clean energy transition. Everyone wins – SolarShare gains the perfect canvas for its solar arrays, and the community benefits from clean energy generation and potentially, revenue-sharing agreements with the landowners.

Harnessing the Sun's Power: Each community solar garden is meticulously equipped with extensive solar panel arrays. These panels act as sunlight collectors, transforming solar energy into electricity. The size and capacity of these gardens are carefully calculated to meet the collective energy needs of the subscribing households within the community. Unlike traditional rooftop installations, which cater to individual needs, community solar gardens are designed with the entire community's energy consumption in mind.

A Chorus of Sunbeams: Powering Your Neighborhood

Imagine a field of gleaming solar panels, working together like a well-rehearsed choir. Each panel acts as a vocalist, capturing the sun's energy and converting it into a harmonious stream of clean electricity. This

symphonic approach eliminates the need for individual rooftop installations in every home. Homes with limited roof space, unfavorable roof angles, or those shaded by trees can finally join the solar energy movement thanks to SolarShare's community garden network.

Bridging the Gap: Short Circuits for Big Savings

Location is a game-changer when it comes to solar power. SolarShare strategically places community solar gardens within the neighborhoods they serve. This creates a **"short circuit"** for clean energy. By minimizing the distance between electricity generation and consumption, SolarShare ensures that the maximum amount of power reaches your home. Reduced transmission distances not only translate to cost savings for you but also contribute to an **eco-friendly energy system**. Less energy loss during transmissions, maximizing the effectiveness of the entire solar power network and minimizing its environmental footprint.

Beyond Generation: A Shared Resource

The beauty of community solar gardens lies not just in generating clean energy, but also in sharing it effectively within the community. SolarShare utilizes innovative practices and cutting-edge technology to ensure a fair and efficient distribution system. Stay tuned to learn more about how SolarShare harnesses the power of these community gardens to bring solar energy directly to your home!

Subscription Model

For a monthly subscription fee, residents can sign up for SolarShare similar to a regular utility payment. More people can now afford solar energy thanks to this concept, which democratizes the access to it.

Subscription, Not Investment: SolarShare is available to residents for a monthly subscription cost that is comparable to a typical utility payment. As a result, the significant upfront cost of installing each solar panel is eliminated.

Financial Accessibility: SolarShare opens up solar energy as a financially viable alternative for more people by using a subscription model. By guaranteeing that access to renewable energy isn't restricted to those with substantial financial means, this "democratizes" the access to it.

Smart Meter Integration

Smart meter-equipped homes monitor their energy use. The real-time energy-sharing component of SolarShare's model depends on this data.

Smart Meter Integration: Powering Transparency and Efficiency

SolarShare has developed an effective and dynamic energy-sharing system by utilizing the capabilities of smart meters. Installed in participating homes, these clever gadgets serve as the system's eyes, continuously monitoring the energy consumption of your family in real time.

Here's how smart meters contribute to SolarShare's success:

Real-Time Data, Real-Time Solutions: A steady stream of information about your energy usage is provided by smart meters. SolarShare's real-time energy-sharing methodology depends on this data. It enables us to precisely estimate the quantity of clean energy your home requires from the community solar garden and guarantees you get the best possible deal.

Transparency is Key: You may easily view the data that smart meters have acquired by using the SolarShare app. This openness builds confidence and gives you the ability to make wise choices about how much energy you use. You can monitor the precise amount of solar energy you use and its contribution to your total energy use.

Optimizing Energy Sharing: SolarShare can continuously improve the energy flow within the community solar garden network thanks to the real-time data from smart meters. Houses that generate more solar energy than they need at any point of time might share it with their neighbors. This dynamic technique reduces waste and guarantees effective energy consumption.

Smart meters are a key element of SolarShare's commitment to a transparent and sustainable energy future. We can create a situation where your energy budget and the environment benefit from using real-time data.

Real-time Energy Sharing

SolarShare is an energy-sharing system that is transparent and safe thanks to its use of blockchain technology. Subscribing families receive the power provided by the community solar garden according to their current requirements.

Real-time distribution: Based on their current needs, subscribing families receive power from the communal solar garden. This guarantees that everyone gets the clean energy they need at any given time.

Localized Energy Grid: SolarShare establishes a community-wide localized energy infrastructure. This encourages the development of a more robust and sustainable energy system by lowering dependency on conventional, centralized power facilities.

SolarShare App: Your Gateway to a Brighter Energy Future

SolarShare is about giving you the power to take charge of your energy use and meanwhile also contribute to a sustainable future. The SolarShare app, your one-stop shop for controlling your solar energy experience, may help with that. The following are some ways that the app's features show the way to a better tomorrow:

Subscription Management

The days of intricate contracts and unstated costs are long gone. You can easily manage your subscription plan, join up for the service, and keep track of your monthly payments using the SolarShare app. You have total transparency over your solar energy contribution and utilization, and so you are always in charge.

Community Hub

The app represents the sense of community that SolarShare cultivates. Connect with your neighbors who are also members of the network of solar gardens. Educate others on sustainable habits, exchange energy-saving advice, and create a network of others who share your enthusiasm for environmental preservation.

Illuminating Insights: Your SolarShare Energy Dashboard

The SolarShare app goes beyond mere functionality; it transforms your smartphone into a personalized energy command center. Imagine a control panel bathed in sunlight, offering a real-time view of the community solar garden's vibrant energy production. Witness firsthand how sunshine is harnessed and converted into clean electricity that powers your neighborhood.

But that's not all! The app unlocks a deeper level of transparency by enabling you to track your individual energy consumption. Gain valuable insights into your household's energy footprint and identify areas for potential optimization. This transparency extends even further, allowing you to visualize how much shared energy you contribute to the grid and how much you receive from your fellow community members. This empowers you to make informed choices about your energy habits and fosters a collaborative spirit within the solar garden network.

SolarShare USP: A P2P Solar Energy Revolution

SolarShare's key innovation is its focus on creating a peer-to-peer (P2P) platform for sharing excess solar energy within communities. This section will delve deeper into this unique selling proposition (USP), highlighting its:

- **Benefits & Uniqueness:**

Solar for All: SolarShare shatters the financial barrier to solar energy by replacing the hefty upfront costs with a familiar, subscription-based model. This opens the door for everyone in the community to join the clean energy revolution, regardless of their initial investment capacity.

Rooftop Freedom: SolarShare liberates homeowners from the constraints of their roof space or orientation. Traditional solar often requires a south-facing roof with ample sunlight, disqualifying many potential users. Community solar gardens, strategically placed by SolarShare, ensure everyone can benefit from solar power, irrespective of their individual roof suitability.

Hyperlocal Energy Network: SolarShare fosters a hyperlocal energy ecosystem. By creating a network of community solar gardens, SolarShare reduces reliance on distant, centralized power plants. This localized energy sharing not only reduces dependence on traditional grids but also potentially lowers overall energy costs for the community.

Sunshine for a Sustainable Future: SolarShare's commitment to solar energy inherently promotes environmental well-being. Increased solar adoption translates to a decrease in greenhouse gas emissions and air pollution, paving the way for a cleaner, healthier tomorrow.

Community Powered by the Sun: SolarShare goes beyond generating clean energy; it cultivates a spirit of community. Their app fosters connections between residents, transforming them into informed solar advocates. This platform allows them to share energy-saving tips, learn about renewable energy advancements, and collectively illuminate a brighter future.

Challenges and Regulations:

- **Initial Investment:** Establishing and maintaining community solar gardens requires a significant initial investment.

- **Grid Integration:** Integrating community solar gardens with existing power grids may require regulatory approvals and infrastructure modifications.

- **Energy Sharing Agreements:** Clear legal agreements need to be established to govern the sharing of excess solar energy between households.

- **Data Privacy:** Data collected by smart meters needs to be handled according to strict data privacy regulations.

SolarShare's P2P model presents a compelling approach to democratizing access to solar energy. However, navigating the technical, regulatory, and legal hurdles will be critical for its widespread adoption.

Knowledge is Sunshine: Empowering You with SolarShare Academy

SolarShare isn't just about delivering clean energy; it's about fostering a community of informed and empowered citizens. That's why the SolarShare app boasts a comprehensive SolarShare Academy, a gateway to a wealth of educational resources. Immerse yourself in the fascinating world of solar energy with engaging articles that demystify the science behind solar power generation and its positive impact on the environment. Learn practical tips and tricks for maximizing energy efficiency in your home, putting real power-saving strategies at your fingertips.

The learning doesn't stop there! The app also offers an in-depth exploration of the benefits of community solar sharing, allowing you to grasp the bigger picture and the positive impact it has on your local environment and community. With SolarShare Academy, you'll gain the knowledge and confidence to make informed decisions about your future energy and become a champion for a cleaner tomorrow.

The SolarShare app is a doorway to a more sustainable future rather than merely a useful tool. Get it now to begin enjoying the benefits of communal solar energy!

SolarShare: Powering Progress, One Community at a Time

SolarShare is a movement as much as a corporation. We think that empowering communities is the first step toward achieving a sustainable future—one that is not just feasible but also doable. Here are some examples of the creative approaches that drive SolarShare's goals:

Building a Sustainable Revenue Model:

- **Subscription Fees:** The monthly subscription fees residents pay form the basis of our business model. As a result, a greater number of individuals may now receive renewable energy because the initial cost barrier associated with traditional solar systems is eliminated.

- **Partnership Power:** SolarShare cultivates strategic alliances with roofing and solar panel installation firms. This results in a win-win scenario. They have access to a useful platform for exhibiting their services, and we help them make connections with prospective clients in the neighborhood.

- **Data-Driven Innovation:** SolarShare is dedicated to ongoing development. An invaluable resource is created from the anonymized and aggregated data on patterns of energy consumption gathered by smart meters. By using this data for research and development, we will be able to improve the effectiveness of community solar sharing and optimize our system. In compliance with stringent data privacy standards, this anonymized data may also be sold to utilities and energy suppliers, giving them useful insights to enhance their services.

Social Impact: A Brighter Future for All

The influence of SolarShare goes beyond financial performance. In the areas we serve, we're dedicated to having a good social impact:

- **Increased Access to Renewable Energy:** SolarShare reduces the initial investment required and lowers the barrier to entry for solar energy. This makes it possible for more homes, no matter how big or little, to take part in the clean energy revolution.

- **Reduced Energy Bills:** For locals, community solar sharing provides a way to save big money. With a SolarShare subscription, you can access affordable, clean, renewable energy, which helps people who need it most by easing the burden of high-power costs.

- **Environmental Benefits:** A sustainable and clean energy source is solar energy. SolarShare helps to reduce greenhouse gas emissions and provides a cleaner future for future generations by encouraging its adoption. Lowering air pollution improves public health in addition to the environment.

- **Community Building:** SolarShare produces more than just renewable electricity. Through the community hub on our app, we encourage residents to connect to develop a feeling of community. Educate others on sustainable habits, exchange energy-saving advice, and create a network of others who share your enthusiasm for environmental preservation. One community at a time, we can work together to build a more sustainable future.

SolarShare is a social movement that entails more than simply solar energy. Come along with us as we blaze the way to a future that is cleaner, brighter, and more interconnected. Together, we can create a future driven by community by utilizing the power of the sun.

SolarShare App: Your Gateway to a Brighter Energy Future

- Imagine Sonia as a modest bungalow-dwelling single mother. She was always stressed out by her skyrocketing power costs, which made it difficult for her to balance putting food on the table and keeping the lights on. She then became aware of SolarShare. She downloaded the app out of curiosity and found a world of opportunities. She quickly cut her monthly energy bills by subscribing to the community solar plan with a few clicks. She was able to keep an eye on her energy usage and even share any excess solar power with her neighbor, Mr. Raghav, a retired teacher living on a fixed income, thanks to the app's interactive dashboard. Sonia feels responsible for the environment and is more financially powerful now. Through the community centre on the app, she establishes connections with other SolarShare users and exchanges energy-saving advice.

- The goal of the SolarShare app is to connect individuals and build a feeling of community, not just to provide functionality. Take Michael as an example. Michael was a young professional with a strong interest in technology and sustainability, but he felt constrained by living in an apartment. He learned about communal solar power through the SolarShare app. He discovered how the software makes use of real-time data to maximize neighborhood energy sharing so that everyone may take advantage of the clean energy produced by the community solar garden. Michael teaches people about renewable energy and the advantages of community solar sharing for the environment by actively participating in the app's forum.

- SolarShare is a platform for change rather than just an app. Consider the Hernandez family's tale. Their massive ranch house was often overrun by electrical bills. They were quite aback to see that their energy expenses had significantly decreased after signing up with SolarShare. They were able to reduce their use even more by adopting energy-saving habits thanks to the app's teaching tools. The Hernandez family now actively engages in neighborhood gatherings that are coordinated via the app, highlighting the advantages of solar power and encouraging others to become part of the SolarShare movement.

- These are just a few instances of how communities and lives are being changed by the SolarShare app. Get the app now to begin enjoying the benefits of communal solar energy!

Join a movement that is about creating a better future together rather than simply focusing on wattage.

Conclusion

The secret to a more sustainable future lies in the great expanse of the sky. SolarShare is about more than simply using the sun; it's about using communal power. In our ideal society, communities would embrace sustainable energy, sharing its abundance and promoting a feeling of shared responsibility, rather than simply companies.

By establishing a network of communal solar gardens, SolarShare upends the conventional solar energy paradigm. Solar-powered, these gardens produce clean electricity that is provided to subscription families according to their current requirements. Thanks to this creative solution, everyone may now get solar energy without having to pay the initial fees associated with individual rooftop installations.

The SolarShare app is a doorway to a better future rather than merely a useful tool. You may interact with your neighbors, keep an eye on your energy use, adjust your subscription, and get information about the advantages of renewable energy all through the app. This encourages a feeling of solidarity and gives you the ability to decide how much energy you use wisely.

SolarShare isn't just another company chasing profits; it's a movement driven by social impact. We're passionate about expanding access to renewable energy sources, bringing down energy costs for communities, and fostering a culture of environmental responsibility. We believe that by working together, brick by brick, neighbor by neighbor, communities can harness the sun's power and illuminate a brighter future, one watt at a time.

Come along for the SolarShare revolution now. Download the app, choose a plan, and begin harnessing the power of solar energy generated locally. Together, let's shine a light on a more sustainable and clean future.

Chapter-7

Redefining Sustainable Fashion with ReVerso

"ReVerso," the brand name, is a combination of "verso" and "reverse." It conveys a transformed outlook towards fashion sustainability, illustrating their mission to revive clothes that were once discarded by granting them another lease on life. The goal lies in transforming people's opinions about used clothing and recognizing its impact as well as possibilities.

Introduction: A fusion of nostalgia and necessity

Have you ever held onto a well-loved yet unworn garment, burdened by the guilt of discarding it but unsure of a sustainable alternative? Or perhaps you've witnessed the overflowing landfills brimming with textile waste, a stark reminder of our society's fast fashion habits. ReVerso, emerges from this confluence of personal memories and a pressing environmental concern. It's a mobile application that addresses the issue of used clothing disposal while rekindling the heartwarming tradition of pre-loved clothing exchange.

Market Research: A Gaping Hole in a Booming Industry

The Indian garment industry is experiencing phenomenal growth, projected to reach a staggering US$250 billion by 2025. This surge is fueled by a growing economy, rising disposable incomes, and a fashion-conscious population. However, this trend has a dark side - a burgeoning problem of textile waste. Traditional methods of disposal, like landfills and incineration, pose significant environmental threats. While online marketplaces exist for pre-loved clothing, they often cater to a specific niche or lack the human touch. ReVerso aims to bridge this gap by offering a comprehensive, user-friendly platform that promotes mindful consumption and fosters a sense of community.

User Pain Points: Emotional sentiments Vs Practicality dilemma

We've all been there - overflowing wardrobes, lingering emotional attachments to old clothes, and the sheer inconvenience of traditional donation methods. Here's a closer look at the user pain points ReVerso addresses:

- **Emotional Disconnect:** Disposing of pre-loved garments can be emotionally taxing, especially when they hold sentimental value.

    ReVerso offers a solution that allows users to give their clothes a new life, ensuring they are cherished by someone else.

- **Lack of Convenience:** Traditional clothing donation often involves time-consuming sorting and drop-offs at charity centres.

  ReVerso provides a seamless pick-up service, eliminating this hassle.

- **Limited Options:** Existing online platforms for pre-loved clothing cater to specific demographics or lack transparency in the resale process.

  ReVerso offers a wider audience and a clear picture of where the clothes are headed.

Solution: A Sustainable Symphony of Reuse and Upcycling

ReVerso goes beyond simply selling used clothes. It's an ecosystem built on three core pillars:

- **Relove and Resale:** Users can sell their pre-loved garments through our platform. We partner with trusted logistics companies to ensure convenient pick-up and delivery. A transparent pricing system, based on garment condition and brand, empowers users to make informed decisions to sell.

- **Upcycling Revolution:** B and C-grade garments, unsuitable for resale, are transformed into something new! We collaborate with NGOs that support skilled artisans, particularly women entrepreneurs, who upcycle these clothes into trendy tote bags or other sustainable products.

- **Conscious Community:** ReVerso fosters a community of environmentally conscious individuals. Users can track the journey of their donated clothes, witnessing their transformation into beautiful upcycled products.

Execution Strategies: Weaving a Seamless User Experience

The ReVerso app will be designed with an intuitive and user-friendly interface. Here's a glimpse into its functionalities:

Effortless Listing: Sell or donate your clothes with ease! Simply upload photos and descriptions, including size and brand details, for a smooth experience.

Fair Value Estimates: Our innovative AI system calculates a transparent price per kilogram based on garment condition and current fashion trends, ensuring a fair exchange.

Seamless Pick-Up: Relax! Partnered logistics providers will schedule convenient doorstep pick-ups of your pre-loved clothing.

Track Your Treasures: Stay informed! With real-time tracking, you'll always know where your clothes are headed, whether for resale or upcycling adventures.

Sustainable Style Community: Connect with like-minded individuals who share your passion for eco-friendly fashion. Discover one-of-a-kind upcycled creations crafted from donated garments – a treasure trove for the conscious shopper!

Revenue Model: A Sustainable Ecosystem that Benefits All

ReVerso's revenue model is designed to ensure financial viability while creating social and environmental impact. Here's how it works:

Resale Commission: A small percentage of the selling price is retained from clothes sold through our platform.

Upcycled Product Sales: Profits from the sale of upcycled products are divided into three parts. One part supports ReVerso operations, the second is distributed among partner NGOs, and the final share empowers the women artisans involved in the upcycling process.

Logistics and Processing Fees: A nominal fee might be applied to cover the costs associated with pick-up, sorting, and processing of donated clothes.

Social Impact: More Than Just a Business

ReVerso isn't just about fashion; it's about fostering positive change. Here's how we're making a difference:

Throttling Textile Trash: ReVerso champions giving clothes a second life through reuse and upcycling. This diverts tons of unwanted garments from landfills, dramatically shrinking the fashion industry's environmental footprint – a major polluter on a global scale.

Empowering Women, Weaving Stronger Communities: ReVerso collaborates with NGOs to empower female artisans, especially those in rural areas. By integrating them into upcycling initiatives, ReVerso offers them a steady source of income, fostering valuable skills and economic independence for these women.

Cultivating a Sustainable Style Ethos: ReVerso sheds light on the environmental repercussions of fast fashion, promoting mindful consumption habits. Our platform, brimming with pre-loved clothing and upcycled creations, inspires a more sustainable approach to fashion – one that seamlessly blends style with environmental consciousness.

App Functionality Enhancements:

- **Search and Filter:** Consider adding robust search and filter options to allow users to easily find desired pre-loved items based on size, brand, style, material, and even color.

- **Condition Rating System:** Implement a clear and consistent condition rating system (e.g., excellent, good, fair) to guide users in pricing their clothes and manage expectations for buyers.

- **Social Sharing and Gamification:** Integrate social sharing buttons to allow users to share their ReVerso finds and promote the platform. Consider incorporating a gamification element by rewarding users with points or badges for selling, donating, or upcycling a certain number of items.

Marketing and User Acquisition Strategies:

- **Targeted Social Media Marketing:** Develop targeted social media campaigns to reach your ideal demographics, which likely include environmentally conscious millennials and Gen Z. Partner with sustainable fashion influencers to promote ReVerso.

- **Collaborations and Partnerships:** Partner with eco-conscious clothing brands or vintage stores to cross-promote each other's platforms and reach new audiences.

Expanding the Upcycling Initiative:

- **Upcycled Product Variety:** Explore expanding the variety of upcycled products offered beyond tote bags. Consider phone cases, accessories, homeware, or even pet products made from recycled textiles.

- **DIY Upcycling Tutorials:** Partner with upcycling artisans to create educational tutorials showcasing how users can upcycle clothes at home, further reducing textile waste.

Building Brand Trust and Transparency:

- **Sustainability Certifications:** Consider pursuing certifications relevant to sustainable practices to demonstrate ReVerso's commitment to environmental responsibility.

- **Partnerships with NGOs:** Showcase the positive impact of your partnerships with NGOs by highlighting the stories and achievements of the women artisans involved in the upcycling process.

Future Vision:

- **Subscription Service:** Explore the possibility of a subscription service offering a curated selection of pre-loved clothing or upcycled items delivered to users' doorsteps periodically.

- **Global Expansion:** As ReVerso gains traction, consider outlining a plan for strategic expansion into new markets with similar needs for sustainable clothing solutions.

Unique Selling Points (USP):

- **Emotional Connection:** We recognize the sentimental importance associated with apparel. ReVerso allows you to give your pre-loved clothes a new life while ensuring they are enjoyed by someone else. **(Emotional USP)**

- **Seamless Upcycling Revolution:** Unlike other marketplaces, we do not end with reselling. Unsellable clothing is repurposed into beautiful goods by talented craftsmen, supporting female entrepreneurs and reducing textile waste. **(Upcycling USP)**

- **Transparent and Empowering:** Our AI-powered pricing system gives you fair value for your goods. You may sell, give, or follow the progress of your items as they are changed. **(Transparency and User Choice USP)**

- **Community of Changemakers:** Join a network of environmentally concerned people who share your enthusiasm for sustainable fashion. Discover innovative upcycled items and inspire others to practice mindful consumption. **(Community and Sustainability USP)**

The Spark: A Story of Need and Connection

Anya, a recent fashion school graduate, stared at the overflowing closet doors in her tiny apartment. Mountains of clothes, unworn and unwanted, stared back. A vintage floral dress, a sequined top from a one-night-out phase, a pair of skinny jeans a size too small – vestiges of trends and impulses, now gathering dust. Guilt gnawed at her. Didn't she just scoff at fast fashion a month ago in her sustainability presentation? Here she was, contributing to the very problem.

As Anya wrestled with her overflowing wardrobe, downstairs, Mrs. Gupta sorted through a worn-out sari. It held memories of her daughter's wedding, a joyous occasion, yet the fabric was fraying. Throwing it away felt disrespectful, but what else could she do?

Across town, Rohan, a young delivery person, cycled past overflowing trash bins, a familiar sight. A discarded T-shirt, with a barely faded superhero logo, tugged at his heart. His younger brother would've loved that. But used clothes were "uncool," and new ones were a luxury they couldn't afford.

The idea for ReVerso struck Anya that night. She envisioned a platform where clothes could find new life, stories could be exchanged, and the environment could breathe a little easier. It wouldn't just be about selling used clothes; it would be about conscious consumption and community.

Anya started small. She listed her unworn clothes on the newly launched ReVerso app. Mrs. Gupta, hesitant but curious, uploaded a picture of her sari, hoping someone could find a new use for it. Rohan, intrigued by the app's mission, downloaded it, a sliver of hope flickering for his brother's birthday gift. The connections began. A young artist bought the floral dress, inspired by its vintage charm. Mrs. Gupta's sari was transformed into a beautiful clutch by a skilled artisan, a story woven into the fabric. Rohan found a gently used superhero shirt, his brother's eyes lit up with joy.

ReVerso wasn't just about clothes; it was about stories finding new chapters. Anya, Mrs. Gupta, Rohan – their lives, once unconnected, were now intertwined by a shared desire for a more sustainable future. The overflowing landfills became a distant worry, replaced by a community fostering conscious living, one garment at a time.

From Toxic Trends to Sustainable Style: ReVerso's Impact

The Fashion Industry's Environmental Shadow-

The fashion industry, while delivering coveted trends, casts a long shadow on the environment. A staggering 20% of global wastewater and 10% of global carbon emissions come from textile production and disposal. This pollution harms ecosystems, wildlife, and human health. Here's where ReVerso steps in, offering a distinctly different approach.

Promoting a Circular Fashion Economy

ReVerso promotes a circular fashion economy, giving pre-loved clothes a second life. This not only reduces the demand for new garments, which require significant resources and energy to produce but also diverts clothing from landfills. Landfills are notorious for methane emissions, a potent greenhouse gas, and textile waste can take hundreds of years to decompose, leaching harmful chemicals into the surrounding environment.

By encouraging mindful consumption and upcycling, ReVerso tackles pollution at its source. Pre-loved clothing finds new owners, unwanted garments are transformed into beautiful upcycled products, and the environmental footprint of fashion shrinks with each item given a second chance. This creates a ripple effect, promoting a more sustainable future for fashion and the planet.

Conclusion: "One garment at a time: a sustainable revolution"

ReVerso was born not just from overflowing closets and overflowing landfills but from a deeper yearning – a need for connection, for purpose, and a more sustainable world.

Anya's overflowing wardrobe sparked a movement, weaving together the stories of strangers through pre-loved clothes and upcycled creations. ReVerso offered a solution not just for unwanted garments, but for a society yearning for mindful consumption and a future where fashion and sustainability could coexist. As ReVerso takes root, its impact transcends individual closets, promising a future where textile waste dwindles, communities connect, and a new chapter in sustainable fashion unfolds.

Chapter-8

Kinaya - Heritagescape: Unveiling the Authentic Tapestry of Asian Landscapes

The term "Kinaya" comes from merging the words "heritage," which denotes a cultural inheritance and passed-down customs, and "scape," associated with panoramic vistas. Therefore, this title represents an initiative committed to conserving and presenting Asia's varied heritage by providing visitors with innovative experiences enriched through technology while engaging local communities in sharing their stories.

Introduction:

When seeking exciting narrative-based authentic as well as engaging travel experiences in Asia, the smartphone hits a significant brick wall because the travel apps' recommended route do not point to those interesting stories and engaging experiences that lie just off the beaten track.

Picture this: one is walking on a serene hillside overlooking magnificent rice fields and stunning temples. Despite the breathtaking scenery, it leaves the traveler detached from something significant. They lack the rich stories behind these houses, the pulse of the local community, and the touch of every living, breathing aspect of the culture, instead of experiencing it only at a 'skin-deep' level. This is a situation common in Asia, which often becomes a tourist trap with similar-looking shops and language barriers making it hard to locate the perfect spot. However, what if there was a chance to decode the essence of this enchanting continent while providing with a genuine representation of cultural introduction and historical safeguarding?

Welcome to Kinaya – one of the most outstanding travel platforms in the world, Kinaya aims to change the model of travelling through Asia. It is not merely an application for tourists but a bold movement for change, supporting endangered traditions and local communities, while also offering a positive light on cultural tourism.

There are 42 UNESCO World Heritage Sites in India, and an additional 57 sites are currently awaiting the prestigious designation. However, these locations hold much more significance than just being popular tourist destinations; they serve as crucial connectors to the country's diverse cultural and natural heritage. One such example is Unakoti in Tripura, known for its captivating rock carvings and stone images that have earned it comparisons to Angkor Wat in the North-East Asia. Despite the surrounding mystery regarding its creators' intentions or purposes of their creation between the 7th and 9th centuries CE), intricate sculptures depict Hindu deities offering invaluable insight into ancient religious practices and artistic traditions from this region lost with time - now forever captured!

The living root bridges of Meghalaya are an astonishing attraction. Rather than being constructed, they grow gradually over many years as the Ficus elastica tree's roots are directed across waterways to create robust, breathing structures. These exceptional formations - some spanning more than 100 feet and able to withstand weighty loads - embody the brilliant techniques for sustainable life created by Khasi and Jaintia locals. They signify a strong link between humans and nature while serving as concrete verification that age-old intelligence can address present-day issues with ease.

Incorporating these sites into Kinaya's selection can significantly enhance the travel experience, enabling tourists to discover India's rich heritage and its wonders. By showcasing both popular and lesser-known locations, Kinaya can contribute towards increasing awareness about preserving culturally significant landmarks. This strategy not only boosts comprehension and admiration for India's varied heritage but also endorses sustainable tourism practices that benefit the local communities.

Data & Statistics: The increased demand for genuine, real, and sincere travel experiences

The need for responsible tourism is not a trend that is unique to certain cultures or countries but one that is felt across the world. A recent study by the World

Tourism Organization revealed that over 60% of people, travel for cultural tourism, a significant increase from 10 years ago. This overwhelming demand highlights the need for Kinaya, a platform capable of delivering the personal, historical travel experiences that the current generation seeks.

Vision Statement:

Innovative solutions enrich communities, protecting cultural identities, and reimagining Asian tourism.

The vision of Kinaya goes beyond software designed for travelling; it encompasses educating and inspiring local populations, reviving and transforming threatened cultural identities, and re-imagining how people of Asia and the wider world may interact with the rich legacy of the region's past. This is what Kinaya aims to achieve – using today's technology to inspire modern travelers and connect them with Asia's vibrant but hidden cultural facets.

Kinaya: Your Gateway to Asia's Hidden Cultural Gems

Market Niche: The Culturally Invested Traveler

Kinaya caters for travelers who seek more than just a selfie at a landmark. They crave off-the-beaten-path experiences, understanding authentic craftsmanship, and interacting with those who preserve Asia's rich cultural heritage.

Filling the Gap in Travel Apps

While travel apps abound, most fail to **fully unlock** the essence of Asian heritage. Existing platforms prioritize mainstream attractions, neglecting the discovery of hidden cultural gems. Additionally, a lack of diverse language support and **meaningful community engagement** hinders genuine connections with local communities.

Opportunities and Challenges: Technology for Preservation

The booming cultural tourism sector in Southeast Asia presents a fertile ground for Kinaya's growth. As travelers seek authentic experiences, the demand for a platform facilitating these interactions rises. Many endangered traditions and sites in the region require urgent protection. Kinaya steps in here.

However, the task is not without challenges. Reaching this audience demands a **concerted and partnership-oriented strategy**. Collaboration with locals, governments, and other stakeholders is crucial to overcome cultural barriers, navigate local bureaucracies, and implement technological solutions. Kinaya needs to involve various stakeholders – local communities, government agencies, and cultural institutions – to tailor solutions that meet everyone's needs.

By addressing these challenges and opportunities, Kinaya can become the go-to app for culturally invested travelers, promoting responsible tourism and preserving Asia's rich heritage for generations to come.

Market Trends:

AI and AR supplementing innovation and Community-based Platforms Remain at the Heart of Every Market.

The travel industry is developing new technologies that alter how tourists interact with their destinations. Kinaya is well-placed to leverage these advanced innovations to provide exquisite experiences for emerging heritage tourists.

AI is also becoming a central figure in the travel industry so that it can help create a more customized trip according to the preferences of the customers. While using AI algorithms integrated into the application and the content posted by other users, Kinaya can also offer travelers individual fountains that reveal exciting stories not visible on the tourist map.

Augmented Reality (AR) technology is also changing the way tourists immerse themselves in historical heritage and cultural attractions. AR overlays in Kinaya will change traditional landmarks into engaging narratives, transporting users back in time.

Kinaya's innovative system of Heritage Hosts will institutionalize a network allowing communities to own and narrate their heritages, fostering authentic interactions rather than scripted ones.

By adopting these innovative trends, Kinaya will revolutionize Asian travel destinations, evolving far beyond typical travel applications.

Unveiling User Pain Points: Bridging the Gap to Authentic Experiences

Unearthing the Hidden Gems:

Cultural anthropology can lead travelers to frustrating dead ends, where every exotic place in Asia has been visited and revisited.

Consider, for example, an adventurous journalist who wants to find modern substitutes for the villainous European merchant and learn about the old methods of tea production in a mountain village in Northern Vietnam. The traveler spends countless hours looking for research materials or even reading numerous online reviews, yet finds little information about this hidden gem. Disappointment sets in as they feel deprived of a genuine Asian experience, and finally, they are confined to the standard tea house that is provided in their hotel.

Bridging the Communication Gap: Language barrier is a significant factor limiting the exploration of the Greater Southeast Asia. Travelers including experts may face difficulties due to language barriers or cultural differences, hindering their ability to negotiate and appreciate the unique aspects of the region. Imagine a traveler in Bali wanting to learn traditional mask carving. Despite their interest, the language barrier prevents meaningful interaction with the local artisans, leaving the traveler dissatisfied and unable to fully experience the craft.

Breaking Free from Tourist Traps: Generic and packaged tourist experiences have 'watered-down' the nature of many important cultural sites in Asia. Travelers often find themselves unable to engage deeply with the culture of their destination, leading to superficial encounters.

For instance, a family visiting a popular temple in Thailand may find the experience marred by large crowds, souvenir shops, and the commercialization of the site, leaving them disappointed and disconnected from the temple's historical and cultural heritage.

Kinaya: A Revolutionary Solution

AI and UGC as the centre of the strategy, Kinaya offers a planned and directed journey experience with the help of advanced AI and user-generated content. The platform's AI-driven algorithms create customized itineraries based on travelers' interests, preferences, and history, ensuring a deeply immersive cultural experience.

For instance, a solo woman traveler interested in traditional artisanal crafts can use Kinaya to discover unique cultural experiences in northern Thailand, from textile factories to ancient pottery processes, which would be otherwise difficult to find.

Augmented Reality Storytelling: Kinaya transcends conventional travel applications, by integrating AR technology, transforming historical landmarks into engaging experiences. Travelers can witness ancient ceremonies and architectural marvels come alive, preserving and sharing Asia's vibrant history. Picture yourself standing before an ornate colonnade in an ancient place in Kyoto, Japan. With a smartphone, AR overlays bring historical scenes to life, allowing travelers to witness royal ceremonies and immerse themselves in the liveliness of history.

Empowering Local Communities: The Heritage Host Network champions the spirit of local people with an emphasis on being the hosts of the cultural heritage. This vision is realized through the community of the special Heritage Hosts – the select group of locals involved in the platform, including artisans, historians and other noblemen of each region who become the curators of the places. Heritage Hosts receive thorough training to welcome visitors, interpret cultural heritage, and manage heritage resources.

Building the Kinaya App: Functionality & Features

Interactive Map: Discovering the Wonders of Asia

Beneath the main attraction is an ultimate treasure map that acts as the key to exploring the gems of Asia. It offers an immersive approach to browsing through the lists of recommended Historical Sites, Artisans, Culinary experiences, or any other brilliant Location shared and recommended by the platform's AI and the Heritage Hosts.

The previously indicated markers, when touched, open a page with a brief description of the spot, its photos and videos, as well as comments by other travelers. The map's ease of use also means that the users can refine it and search for specific areas of interest like cultural and historical destinations, folk arts and crafts, or local dishes, ensuring a personalized journey.

AR-Powered Tours: Exploring Kinaya through Time

The application's strongest feature is the use of AR technology that allows users to experience time-based travel as they scan historical monuments and cultural centres. All they have to do is to aim the vitality of their smartphone to a certain point of interest and the users will see a historically accurate AR layer.

Whether watching a ceremonial procession in front of a palace, artisans at a craft centre, or exploring a temple's details, the experience rivets users to a prospective world presenting a special sense of familiarity with the historic past.

Community Hub: Engaging the Heritage Hosts and Booking Curated Experiences

The core of Kinaya and Heritage Hosts is an active community of people with heritage experiences and best practices in organic living, where you can communicate and plan unforgettable journeys. Travelers can browse profiles of the potential Heritage Hosts who present expertise, profound knowledge of the place and nationality, as well as love for tradition and history. When users browse through such profiles or make friends online and perhaps, shift to direct messaging, they are in fact, laying the viable groundwork for profound transformations.

Kinaya exposes these experiences through the community hub which also provides a space where one can book for various activities, artisanal hands-on workshops, cooking classes, tours and workshops led by our Heritage Hosts. In a way, there are two sides to it: On one hand, the user has control over choosing the bookings, thus having the structure of the app to have them build the travel experience around their desire to immerse themselves in the cultural landscape.

Additionally, other discussions continue to take place at the community hub where users, the hosts or Heritage Hosts, and other individuals in the Kinaya platform interact. The forums and messaging capabilities, as well as the content selection, let travelers and concerned individuals participate in discussions regarding the sustainable use of the tourism industry, conservation, and the changing management of Asian historical treasures. This symphony of numerous entities not only improves the quality of the service received by the end consumer but also increases the potential durability and usefulness of the site.

Sustainable Revenue & Social Impact: A Balanced Approach

Sustainable Revenue Model: Earning the Win-Win Solution

Kinaya has developed a viable economic model whereby the company will gain all the Revenues required for its operation and expansion while at the same time offering all the necessary support and opportunities for the locals in the respective locations. Pivoting around this framework is a commission-based compensation model that requires the platform to receive a predetermined percentage of gross sales from the app-derived bookings for on-demand Host-led Heritage tours and other culturally infused interactions.

This model makes it possible for Kinaya to continue sourcing for the financial capital that may be needed in the future in the development of more enhanced technological supports, expanding the geographical base of the firm and putting in place the other operational supports that may be required in the attainment of the goal of offering a revolutionary user experience while at the same time guaranteeing that the vast majority of the income flows right back to the local communities. Kinaya pays due attention to the problem of optimizing the overall value accrual of all the stakeholders involved and creates a win-win situation for the company and the context of further activity, which is the protection of the Asian cultural heritage.

Premium Features: Enhancing User Experience

To make Kinaya special and attractive to users, this platform includes additional revenue models offering premium features. These features cater to customers eager for exclusive experiences, such as specially curated guided tours via Heritage Hosts' workshops, specialist itinerary planning by heritage professionals, and augmented reality enhancements that delve into deeper historical narratives of landmarks.

These luxury services allow Kinaya to supplement its operations, fulfilling its mission while satisfying the demands of high-end, culturally aware users. This dual approach allows the platform to stay both financially viable and also committed to making information available to everyone while empowering communities.

Social Impact Measurement: Monitoring the Result and Promoting Sustainable Cultural Tourism Development

. To monitor and augment the platform's effectiveness and create a sustainable growth model at Kinaya, the executive team will put in place a system for assessing KPIs and social impact.

Using a Scopus-based approach, the platform tracks its bottom-up impact, including local people's economic returns, new employment opportunities, and the preservation of historical art forms and practices. Furthermore, Kinaya shall use this information to engage policymakers to consider new policies that enhance the physical bond between cultural conservation and tourism advancement.

By reporting the social issues addressed through the platform, Kinaya not only promotes sustainable travel but also helps shift the general perception of the tourism industry and Asian heritage.

Cultural Preservation: A Moral Imperative
Endangered Traditions: Protecting Asia's Cultural Fabric

In contemporary Asia, spanning vast territories and differing significantly in climate, geological structure and history, a rich fabric of a historical culture hovers on the edge of the rise of the contemporary world and globalized tendencies. From preserving the delicate fabrics woven by Vietnam's hill tribes to understanding the intricate designs of the Philippines' Indigenous people, Kinaya is dedicated to keeping these cultural threads alive.

Kinaya empowers local communities to take responsibility for preserving their identity, creating a bottom-up cultural renaissance. Through Heritage Hosts, the platform connects travelers with cultural ambassadors—artisans, elders, and community members who share their skills and stories, generating sustainable income and fostering pride and conservation of cultural assets.

Advanced technologies, for example, augmented reality and interactive multimedia, give a modern impression to these endangered traditions, which in turn enables the younger generation with advanced technological skills to embrace the programs. Thus, Kinaya not only helps fill in for the lack of connection between the culture of the past and the present but also keeps the spirit of Asian culture alive for present generations and those that may come into the future.

Sustainable Tourism: Redefining the Traveler's Role

Kinaya not only searches or documents the existence of cultural entities but also empowers them to gain viability and function properly. The platform also aims to transform travelers, from passive spectators to active participants in conserving Asia's history and culture.

Connecting users with local communities as members of the Heritage Host network also makes users of the site responsible for proponents of sustainable tourism. From workshops, live simulations, discussion sessions and other practical sessions, the traveler is educated on the various issues that the concerned cultures have to go through to protect their identity.

Kinaya's business strategy focuses on sustainability, reinvesting a significant share of income back into local societies to support cultural heritage projects. This integrated approach positions Kinaya as a leader in ethical travel and cultural engagement.

Empowering the Next Generation: Youth Environmental Education

Kinaya envisions a cultural renaissance that empowers future generations to take charge of preserving and promoting their heritage. It ensures that men and women of a young age empower the local communities and thus relight the cultural identity of Asians and let them develop a proper pride in their heritage and traditions.

Both direct educational schemes, vocational training and mentorship that are supported by the Heritage Host network, will empower the young generation as the rightful heirs and protectors of their cultural heritage which will be promoted by Kinaya. These approaches guarantee that the cultural value of Asians', as well as histories, are preserved for generations to come and are not only relevant but also continue to expand to accommodate the Asian generation in the modern world.

Future technologies like augmented reality and interactive digital platforms appeal to the youth, hence creating interest in the cultures and bridging the gap between the past and the future. This revival encourages continued protection and transmission of cultural values to future generations.

Kinaya: A Transformative Vision for the Future of Asian Travel

In a world increasingly dominated by globalization, which often erases the unique features of Asian regions, Kinaya offers a tool for change.

While the postmodern, global culture threatens to flatten the world into a monocultural space with identical mainland money cultures, shopping malls, food courts, and uninformed masses, Kinaya acts as an emancipatory, utopian vision for putting the regions' local populations back into the cultural practice of travel. With its apropos technology, keen focus on providing a transportive experience, and rapidly solidifying stance on sustainable tourism, the platform has the potential to change how the world appreciates the elaborate heritage of Asia's culturally diverse destinations.

Kinaya's Unique Selling Proposition: Empowering Cultural Custodians and Transforming the Traveler's Experience

Kinaya emerges as a groundbreaking digital platform that offers a dynamic way to experience Asian culture. Its unique selling proposition is a strong focus on the exploration of the idea that the voices of local communities should be the primary source telling their own stories, and a radical shift from the conventional transformative travel experience, in which travelers are offered guided tours through a kaleidoscope of culturally diverse and heritage-rich Asian experiences.

Celebrating Local Talent of Communities

Another key aspect that differentiates Kinaya is the concept of Heritage Hosts which aims to act as a bridge by providing an opportunity for artisans, elders and other prominent and talented personalities of the community to come forward and let the like-minded tourists from the world know about their talent, field expertise and traditional knowledge. Thus, it remains for Kinaya to extend an invitation to the locals, to empower them to be the main storytellers and guides, and in the process, ensure that this wealth of cultural history doesn't just remain buried in the archives but is also propagated to an international audience.

As for Kinaya's unique selling proposition, it focuses not only on the locals but also on the traveler – and on reinventing their approach to the travelling and sightseeing experience so that they become guardians of Asia's cultural heritage rather than mere onlookers. Thus, through the interaction of users with direct enactors Heritage Hosts, travelers can participate in workshops, cultural activities, and meaningful discussions, as well as get acquainted with the problems and perspectives of these communities.

Lastly, Kinaya as a concept is centered on the idea of offering clients the technological side and cultural importance of preservation, along with the concept of sustainable tourism, and the community being a primary stakeholder in the process of preserving heritage and becoming travelers themselves in a way where the process of visiting a historic place is replaced with the experience of a journey, where the traveler becomes a part of something much bigger and ultimately contributes to the positive change. By transcending the established rules of engagement of the traditional travel firms and tour operators and serving as a model for other firms in the tourism industry, the platform revolutionizes the relationship between visitors and destinations by inspiring the culture of responsible tourism and travel.

Beyond the Tourist Trail: Maya's Journey into the Heart of Thailand with Kinaya

The bright neon city of Bangkok became hazy, and Maya sat with her phone, scrolling aimlessly, loneliness enveloping her. Thanks to another generic tour, there is another group of people who are taking selfies with a stick, which is completely fine. But Maya yearned for something far more profound, the spirit of Thailand where the locals live and not the illusion that one sees from a fast car.

Disappointment gnawed at her. And then on a notification, an advertisement for Kinaya appeared. Curiosity truly is the mother of invention; she decided to give it a try and downloaded the app. Pictures of prehistoric buildings, beautiful, calm hamlets and happy people different to any persona in the typical package tour ads filled the screen. This wasn't the Thailand of the travel brochures or Lonely Planet books or National Geographic – the country that tourists and most of the Western world already knew. This was it. She no longer had any doubt in her mind this was legitimate since there were no way debunkers would willingly or knowingly aid me in my research.

This enabled her to interact with Khun Yai, a weaver in one of the most isolated villages in northern Thailand. During their video call, Khun Yai's charming smile and sparkling eyes invited Maya to come and learn the traditional Thai silk weaving technique firsthand. Khun Yai enthusiastically explained how balloon tours work: night, sunrise, balloon, tour. Enchanted by Khun Yai's enthusiasm and eager for an authentic experience, Maya booked the tour.

The journey was strenuous. She followed Kinaya's recommended route which took her through winding roads and lush vegetation that was a contrast to the busy city sounds. The scent of plumeria flowers drifted in the air and the stench of automobile emissions of Bangkok has replaced the once fresh and cool smell of flowers. As soon as Khun Yai met Maya, she invited her into the wooden house, which was a part of their Thai house. The room still held the heady aroma of natural dyes, and the steady click of the loom's pedal provided a soothing, almost hypnotizing auditory accompaniment to Maya's captivation.

The following day, Maya successfully gets Personal Training in silk making. Maya's initial awkwardness was patiently helped by Khun Yai as the bright colors of the threads came alive under her hands. From such actions, Khun Yai shared the problems with her village –young generations who relocated to the city, and textiles by other firms which threatened to overrun their traditional way of weaving. Maya understood now. This wasn't merely about the scarf, but it was also about ownership of identity, of retaining culture, values and traditions inherited from previous generations. Out of the wreckage came a new kind of hope, a kind that made her feel she had a purpose again.

When Maya left the village, she took many lessons with her, but more than anything else she took a souvenir. She wore a stained and hand-woven silk scarf, and she possessed the heart of a thankful and proud Thai woman. What was now evident was that a link had been created and a one-way bridge constructed by Kinaya. Neon signs in Bangkok were no longer ominous but an enchanting variation of the city's previously demoralizing uniformity Bangkok came into focus as a synthesis of what was seen, heard, and smelled. Maya now realized well that these were only the initial days of her Asian tours, thanks to Kinaya and other exciting narratives lying hidden.

Conclusion

In an age where globalization threatens to erase Asia's unique and diverse cultural inheritances, Kinaya offers a glimmer of hope, as the new means of liberating its people and turning travelers into active players-cultural ambassadors in their own right.

Taking a closer look at the strategies implemented in Kinaya, one cannot fail to acknowledge its focus on the critical features of Asian heritages, emphasizing their vulnerability and importance. Leveraging novel technologies, the platform blends the virtual reality of the tourist with the real-life narratives and personalities of local professionals, craftsmen, and community members. This model ensures that these cultural keepers earn a sustainable income while discovering the pride and motivation in witnessing that their culture is preserved.

Kinaya is not only about empowering locals; it also repositions travelers from mere spectators to active participants in the heritage preservation of Asia. By connecting users directly with the Heritage Hosts, the platform allows travelers to become involved in production activities, participate in hands-on workshops, and come up with engaging discussions that enhance users' understanding of the various difficulties and opportunities experienced by hosts.

While globalization poses a risk of homogenizing experiences worldwide, reducing them to standardized accommodations and lifestyles, Kinaya demonstrates that cultural heritage cannot be erased. Through its technology, curated experiences, and commitment to sustainable tourism, Asia's cultural heritage will remain extraordinarily diverse and vibrant as the communities are encouraged to share their stories and traditions through the platform.

Chapter-9

Revolutionizing Access to Affordable and Accessible Healthcare: The Vision of Plansurge.com

Introduction

The platform's fundamental purpose, reflected in its name "Plansurge.com," is to simplify the organization of surgeries. The term "Plan" signifies a methodical and deliberate approach to scheduling procedures while "Surge" represents positive transformations that quickly take place within healthcare services. Thus, when combined, "Plansurge" is an objective towards providing effective surgical care with ease of access, quality assurance and informed decision-making for patients.

In a world where surgical interventions significantly impact healthcare outcomes; a glaring disparity persists. Approximately 31 crore surgeries are performed globally each year, and a substantial portion of the world's population lacks access to these life-saving treatments. According to World Bank report, 14.3 crore additional surgical procedures are needed each year to save lives and prevent disability. This unmet need translates easily manageable conditions into fatal diseases. The situation is mirrored in India, where high costs and inadequate healthcare accessibility, especially in rural areas, create significant barriers to planned surgeries, leading to dire health consequences.

Here's a deeper exploration of this issue with real data:

Global Perspective

- According to a report by The Lancet Commission on Global Surgery, an estimated 31 crore surgeries are performed worldwide annually. However, this number varies widely by region and income level. Low- and middle-income countries (LMICs) often face significant challenges in accessing surgical care.

- The Lancet Commission highlighted that over 5 billion people worldwide lack access to safe, affordable surgical and anesthesia care when needed. This lack of access contributes to avoidable deaths and disabilities from treatable surgical conditions.

Indian Healthcare Landscape

- In India, a substantial portion of the population faces obstacles in accessing essential surgical interventions, especially in rural areas. According to the National Health Profile 2019, there were approximately 49 lakh surgeries conducted in India in 2018-19.

- The rural-urban disparity in surgical care access is stark. A significant portion of the rural population faces barriers due to inadequate healthcare infrastructure, limited availability of specialist doctors, and financial constraints.

- The cost factor is a major impediment. Many planned surgeries, including procedures related to proctology, urology, dental, ophthalmology, and laparoscopy, pose financial challenges for a large segment of the population. Essential surgeries such as C-sections, hernia repairs, cataract removals, and gallbladder surgeries remain unaffordable for many.
- The National Sample Survey Office (NSSO) reported that a considerable percentage of hospitalizations in India result in significant out-of-pocket expenditures, leading to financial distress for families, particularly in rural areas.

Impact of Inadequate Access

- The lack of access to timely surgical care often results in manageable conditions progressing into severe and life-threatening diseases. Delays in essential surgeries complicate health conditions, impacting individuals' quality of life and, in severe cases, leading to increased mortality rates.
- Rural communities face challenges such as long travel distances to healthcare facilities, lack of transportation, and insufficient infrastructure, further delaying or preventing access to essential surgical interventions.

The disparity between the availability of surgical interventions and the population's access to these life-saving treatments is evident, both globally and specifically in countries like India. The situation demands a concerted effort to bridge the gaps in healthcare infrastructure, accessibility, and affordability, especially in underserved rural areas. Addressing these issues is crucial to ensuring that individuals receive timely and necessary surgical care, preventing easily treatable conditions from escalating into fatal diseases.

Understanding the Challenge

The World Bank Report underlines the urgency, indicating a need for an additional 14.3 crore surgeries annually worldwide to prevent disabilities and save lives. In India, the landscape of healthcare access is marked by the daunting expense of planned surgeries, rendering procedures in proctology, urology, dental, ophthalmology, laparoscopy, and more unattainable for a significant segment of the population.

The National Health Profile data underscores the persistent struggle for adequate healthcare facilities and services in India. The high out-of-pocket expenditures associated with medical treatments, including surgeries, continue to burden a significant percentage of the population, particularly those in economically weaker sections.

The impact of cost barriers leads to delayed interventions or avoidance of necessary treatments, exacerbating health conditions among individuals. This delay often results in manageable health issues progressing to advanced stages, which can lead to increased complications, disabilities, or even fatalities.

The pressing need to address financial barriers hindering access to essential surgical procedures in

India cannot be overstated. While strides have been made by the government and healthcare organizations to enhance accessibility and affordability, significant segments of the population still struggle to avail themselves of necessary surgical care. Bridging these gaps is imperative to ensure universal access to timely and critical surgical interventions, ultimately preventing avoidable disabilities and saving lives.

The Predicament Faced

The core challenge lies in the prohibitive costs that dissuade patients from pursuing necessary surgeries. Compounded by the need to take time off work and the absence of quality healthcare in their vicinity, individuals often delay or entirely overlook planned surgeries. This delay escalates health conditions, transforming manageable illnesses into life-threatening situations. Moreover, secondary care surgeries pose an increased risk of infection and disease progression due to delayed interventions.

Introducing Plansurge.com: A Solution-Oriented Platform

Plansurge.com emerges as a solution, aiming to democratize healthcare access by making planned surgeries both accessible and affordable for every Indian citizen. This innovative platform operates as a bridge between patients and healthcare providers, revolutionizing the way medical care is accessed and delivered. By leveraging cutting-edge technology and a user-centric interface, Plansurge.com aspires to democratize access to planned surgeries, transcending barriers of geography, economic constraints, and inadequate health infrastructure. It envisions a paradigm shift where the need for essential surgical interventions no longer remains elusive due to financial disparities or limited healthcare resources. Plansurge.com operates as an indispensable bridge between patients and an extensive network of reputable healthcare providers, ensuring a seamless journey from the initial selection of surgery to the finalization of healthcare providers, all within a digitally driven, transparent ecosystem.

The Platform's Functionality

Patients commencing their journey on Plansurge.com start by selecting their desired surgery and a tentative date via the user-friendly application. Following this, they securely upload their medical records, past history, and prescriptions. Once uploaded, the platform disseminates this information across a network of registered hospitals and doctors. Consequently, medical service providers craft quotations tailored to individual patient details, allowing patients to thoroughly review and compare multiple quotes before making an informed decision. Additionally, patients receive complimentary OPD and second opinion consultations, with fees refundable if they opt to proceed with the surgery through the same service provider. Moreover, leveraging patient data, our app assists service providers in developing infrastructure in deficient areas. By aggregating available data, if multiple patients require the same surgery in a town, doctors can plan visits for performing surgeries locally, reducing the need for patients to travel to metro cities for treatments. Recognizing the challenges in accessing specialized treatments like In-Vitro Fertilization (IVF), especially in rural and semi-urban areas, Plansurge.com is committed to closing this gap. Our goal is to empower individuals by providing equitable pathways to vital fertility treatments, regardless of their geographic limitations, thereby addressing discrepancies in reproductive healthcare access. A detailed explanation of how the functionality of Plansurge.com works:

- **User-Friendly Application**

Plansurge.com offers a user-friendly and intuitive application interface accessible via web or mobile devices. Patients initiate their journey by creating an account or logging in to the platform.

- **Selecting Desired Surgery and Tentative Date**

Within the application, patients can browse through various surgical procedures categorized based on specialty or type. They select the type of surgery they require, such as hernia repair, cataract surgery, or dental procedures. Additionally, they can indicate a preferred or tentative date for the surgery.

- **Secure Upload of Medical Records and History**

After choosing the surgery type and date preferences, patients securely upload their medical records, including past history, prescriptions, diagnostic reports, and any other relevant documents. Plansurge.com employs robust encryption and security measures to ensure the confidentiality and integrity of the uploaded data.

- **Dissemination to Registered Hospitals and Doctors**

Plansurge.com functions as an intermediary, transmitting the uploaded medical records and patient requirements to its network of registered hospitals, clinics, and specialist doctors associated with the platform. This network encompasses various healthcare providers with expertise in the specific surgery chosen by the patient.

- **Localized Surgeries**

The platform utilizes patient data to assist service providers in enhancing infrastructure in underserved areas. When multiple patients require similar surgeries, doctors can schedule visits to perform surgeries locally, reducing the need for patients to travel to metropolitan areas for medical procedures.

- **Quotation Preparation by Medical Service Providers**

Upon receiving the patient's details and surgical requirements, the registered medical service providers review the uploaded records and prepare quotations. These quotes are tailored to the individual patient's needs, considering factors like the complexity of the procedure, required hospital stay, surgeon's fees, and other associated costs.

- **Review and Comparison of Quotes**

Patients receive multiple quotations from different medical service providers within the Plansurge.com network. They can thoroughly review and compare these quotes, considering various aspects such as pricing, hospital facilities, surgeon's credentials, location, and any additional services offered.

- **Informed Decision-Making**

Armed with comprehensive information from various quotes, patients can make an informed decision based on their preferences. They might prioritize factors like affordability, reputation of the hospital or surgeon, proximity to their location, or specific facilities offered by different healthcare providers.

- **Selection and Engagement with Chosen Healthcare Provider**

After careful consideration, patients can select the healthcare provider that best aligns with their preferences and requirements. Plansurge.com facilitates the connection between the patient and the chosen provider, enabling further communication, scheduling, and preparation for the surgery.

In essence, Plansurge.com streamlines the process of selecting and obtaining quotes for planned surgeries, empowering patients with information and choices while connecting them with reputable healthcare providers. This ensures a transparent and patient-centric approach to healthcare access.

Advantages of Plansurge.com

Accessibility to Quality Healthcare: The platform ensures accessibility to high-quality medical care for planned surgeries, irrespective of geographical constraints.

Affordable Healthcare via Transparent Pricing: Plansurge.com introduces a quote-based system, ensuring cost transparency and affordability for patients.

Free Consultations: Patients receive complimentary OPD and second opinion consultations, with the fees refundable if they proceed with the surgery through the same service provider.

Informed Choices: Patients can choose healthcare service providers based on comprehensive credentials, reviews, and ratings available on the platform.

Streamlined Medical Records: The platform maintains digitized medical records accessible to patients and doctors, eliminating record-keeping complexities and reducing duplication.

Optimal Resource Utilization: Plansurge.com employs machine learning and AI-driven data analytics to optimize the utilization of medical infrastructure, particularly benefitting rural and semi-urban areas.

Revenue Model and Sustainability

The platform's revenue model is built on revenue sharing with healthcare service providers, charges for medical record maintenance and sharing, collaborations with pharmacies, and advertising revenues, ensuring both viability and scalability. Below is an elaboration on the revenue model of Plansurge.com, which focuses on sustainability through various revenue streams:

- **Revenue Sharing with Healthcare Service Providers**

Plansurge.com engages in a partnership model with hospitals, clinics, and healthcare practitioners wherein a portion of the fees charged for surgeries facilitated through the platform is shared. This mutually beneficial arrangement incentivizes healthcare providers to offer competitive prices while ensuring their visibility and access to a broader patient base.

- **Charges for Medical Record Maintenance and Sharing**

The platform may institute nominal fees for maintaining and sharing digitized medical records securely. This service streamlines the healthcare process by providing a centralized repository accessible to both patients and healthcare professionals. The convenience and security offered by this feature can justify a nominal charge.

- **Collaborations with Pharmacies**

Plansurge.com can establish collaborations with pharmacies to facilitate medication procurement post-surgery. Collaborations may involve exclusive discounts or offers for patients who have undergone surgeries through the platform. In return, the platform could receive a commission or revenue percentage from pharmacy sales driven through the platform.

- **Advertising Revenues**

Leveraging its user base and targeted healthcare audience, Plansurge.com can offer advertising space to various healthcare-related businesses or complementary services, encompassing pharmaceutical companies, medical equipment suppliers, life insurance providers, Mediclaim insurers, and health and wellness products. Revenue generation can be diversified through sponsored content, banner ads, featured listings, and partnerships with Mediclaim insurers and life insurance companies, thereby broadening the platform's offerings and bolstering its revenue streams.

- **Subscription or Membership Model**

Introducing premium features or a subscription-based model for patients or healthcare providers seeking additional services could be an avenue for generating recurring revenue. This could include access to exclusive consultations, priority scheduling, or enhanced visibility on the platform for healthcare providers.

- **Financial Aid providers**

Collaboration and partnerships with financial aid providers such as banks, NBFCs, insurance companies, and NGOs to offer financial assistance, loans, or special funding schemes for patients requiring planned surgeries, generating revenue through facilitation fees or commissions

- **Commission on Additional Services**

Apart from surgeries, Plansurge.com could extend its services to include post-operative care, rehabilitation, or telemedicine consultations. For such services facilitated through the platform, a commission or service fee could be levied, ensuring an extended revenue stream beyond surgical procedures.

- **Data Analytics and Insights**

Plansurge.com could offer anonymized, aggregated data insights to healthcare institutions or research organizations for research purposes. The platform's data could be valuable for trend analysis, healthcare planning, or improving healthcare infrastructure. This could be monetized through subscription-based access or one-time data access fees.

By diversifying revenue streams and creating value-added services around its core offering of facilitating planned surgeries, Plansurge.com ensures a sustainable business model. This multipronged approach not only ensures financial viability but also fosters continuous innovation and expansion of services, ultimately benefiting both patients and healthcare providers.

Plansurge.com stands at the forefront of healthcare evolution, driving a transformative shift in India's medical landscape. By democratizing access to essential healthcare, Plansurge.com envisions a future where every individual receives the medical care they need, nurturing a society that thrives on health equity and well-being. Plansurge.com represents more than just a platform; it embodies a revolutionary leap in India's healthcare narrative. It's a catalyst for change, redefining how healthcare is accessed and experienced. By offering a seamless and transparent pathway to planned surgeries, we are reshaping the very essence of healthcare. Our vision envisages a society where healthcare is not a luxury but an essential right for every individual, fostering a community thriving on the principles of health equity and well-being.

Chapter: 10

EmShe: Empowering Confidence - The Skillshare for Women in STEM

The EmShe brand name comes from the phrase 'Empower She,' underlining its aim to encourage women in STEM fields. It represents inclusivity, confidence, and community among females in science, technology, engineering, and mathematics. The concept behind EmShe is to eliminate boundaries and cultivate an encouraging environment where women can flourish by redefining the field of STEM.

Introduction

The fields of Science, Technology, Engineering, and Mathematics (STEM) fields are brimming with innovation and discovery. However, despite significant progress, women remain underrepresented in these critical sectors. This chapter explores the need for a groundbreaking platform specifically designed to empower women in STEM by fostering confidence, building essential skills, and cultivating a support community.

1. The Current Landscape: Challenges and Opportunities

A. Historical Context and Underrepresentation

Pioneering women like Ada Lovelace, Marie Curie, Katherine Johnson, and Fei-Fei Li paved the way for future generations yet, their stories highlight the persistent struggle for recognition and opportunity in a historically male-dominated field.

B. Statistics and Representation Gaps

Current statistics reveal a concerning picture: women comprise only 28% of the computer science workforce and 13% of engineers in the United States. (https://ncwit.org/) This underrepresentation hinders innovation and limits the potential impact of STEM advancements.

C. Challenges Faced by Women in STEM

Beyond underrepresentation, women in STEM face numerous challenges throughout their careers. These include:

- **Implicit Bias:** Unconscious stereotypes and prejudices regarding women's capabilities in STEM fields can hinder their professional advancement.

- **Lack of Support Systems:** The absence of female mentors and role models can leave women feeling isolated.

- **Gender Pay Gap:** Women in STEM consistently earn less than their male counterparts performing similar work.

- **The Imposter Syndrome:** A recent KPMG study found that many women in STEM often struggle with imposter syndrome and a lack of visible female role models, making it difficult to see themselves succeeding in these fields.

- **The "Leaky Pipeline" Phenomenon:** Research shows a significant decline in the number of women pursuing STEM careers at various stages of the educational and professional pipeline.

2. **Building a Platform for Change**

The proposed platform addresses these challenges by creating a comprehensive and supportive ecosystem for women in STEM. Here's how it will empower women to thrive:

A. Curated Content by Women in STEM

- **Content Types and Structure:** The platform offers a diverse range of content, including lectures, workshops, webinars, interactive coding challenges, and project-based learning experiences. They cater to different learning styles and career goals.

- **Instructor Profiles:** The platform features profiles of accomplished women in STEM, highlighting their professional backgrounds and contributions. This provides valuable role models and showcases the vast array of career paths available within STEM fields.

B. Fostering a Supportive Community

- **Interactive Features:** The platform integrates discussion forums, study groups, and virtual meetups to foster connections and facilitate peer-to-peer learning. This allows women to share experiences, ask questions, and offer support to one another.

- **Success Stories:** The platform showcases success stories of women who have used the platform to advance their careers, secure dream jobs, or launch their own businesses. These stories inspire and motivate users, demonstrating the platform's positive impact.

3. Unique Selling Points: Empowering Women Beyond Skills

While offering high-quality learning resources is essential, the platform goes beyond traditional skills training. Here are some key differentiators:

- **Building Confidence Through Representation:** Curated video profiles of accomplished women will showcase diverse career paths and achievements. These profiles will delve into the personal journeys and challenges faced by these role models, fostering a sense of connection and relatability.

- **Cultivating a Growth Mindset:** The platform integrates gamified elements like coding challenges, virtual labs, and project-based learning with leaderboards and badges. This fosters a sense of accomplishment and motivates users to continuously learn and improve their skills.

- **Championing Advocacy and Allyship:** The platform will host regular interviews with industry leaders, policymakers, and diversity advocates. These discussions will address current issues within STEM workplaces, explore strategies for promoting gender equality, and offer practical advice for overcoming implicit bias. Additionally, an Ally Toolkit will equip allies, both men and women, with the knowledge and tools to advocate for their female colleagues.

4. Building a Collaborative Ecosystem

Beyond offering high-quality learning resources, the platform fosters a supportive ecosystem that empowers women to overcome challenges and achieve their full potential.

- **Fostering Community Through Shared Experiences:** The platform offers themed discussion in forums dedicated to specific STEM disciplines, career stages, and even identity-based groups. This allows women to connect with peers who share their unique experiences and challenges, fostering a sense of belonging and camaraderie. Additionally, mentorship circles will provide personalized guidance and support, allowing women to learn from a diverse range of mentors and benefit from peer-to-peer connections.

- **Prioritizing Mental Wellbeing:** Recognizing the unique pressure faced by women in STEM, the platform will curate resources promoting mental health and well-being. This could include guided meditations, yoga tutorials, or access to online therapy resources. Furthermore, a clear and comprehensive safe space policy will be established, ensuring all users feel comfortable and respected when participating in discussions or online communities.

- **Celebrating Achievements and Milestones:** A virtual recognition wall will allow users to celebrate each other's achievements, big or small. This could include completing a challenging course, landing a new job, or receiving a promotion. Public recognition fosters a sense of community and motivates users to keep pushing forward. Additionally, a dedicated blog section will showcase user-generated content. Women can share their personal stories, career journeys, and technical skills through articles, tutorials, or even creative projects. This not only empowers women to become leaders within the platform but also provides valuable content for other users.

5. A Sustainable Business Model

The platform will utilize a freemium model to ensure accessibility while generating revenue for continued growth and development.

- **Free Membership:** This tier offers access to a limited selection of courses, basic community features, and previews of premium content.

- **Premium Membership:** This tier provides full access to the course library, exclusive career development workshops, priority mentorship matching, advanced learning tools, and additional community features.

6. Building a Strong Team and Advisory Boards

The success of the platform hinges on a dedicated and passionate team with expertise in education, technology, and women's empowerment. Additionally, two advisory boards will be established to ensure the platform remains relevant and impactful.

- **Content Advisory Board:** A distinguished Content Advisory Board will comprise leading women in STEM from academia, industry, and non-profit organizations. This board will guide curriculum development, identify emerging trends, and ensure content reflects the diverse needs of users.

- **Diversity, Equity, and Inclusion (DE&I) Council:** A dedicated DE&I Council will advise on strategies for promoting inclusivity within the platform and the broader STEM community. This council will address accessibility features, content moderation for marginalized identities, and partnerships with organizations that support women of color, LGBTQ+ and women with disabilities in STEM.

7. A Force for Change: The Future of the Platform

The proposed platform is more than just an online learning platform; it's a movement for change. Empowering women in STEM with the skills, confidence, and support system they need, has the potential to revolutionize the landscape of STEM fields and create a ripple effect that benefits society as a whole. Here are some ways the platform can achieve this:

- **Fostering Innovation:** A more diverse and inclusive STEM workforce will lead to a broader range of perspectives and problem-solving approaches. This can lead to groundbreaking innovations across various fields, from healthcare and clean energy to artificial intelligence and space exploration.

- **Inspiring the Next Generation:** The platform's success stories and profiles of accomplished women in STEM can serve as powerful inspiration for young girls considering STEM careers. This can help close the gender gap early on and create a pipeline of future female leaders in science and technology.

- **Addressing Global Challenges:** Many of the world's most pressing challenges, such as climate change, food security, and sustainable development, require solutions rooted in STEM fields. By empowering more women to contribute their talents and expertise, the platform can help accelerate progress towards a more equitable and sustainable future for all.

Future Developments

- **Virtual Reality (VR) Labs:** Providing immersive learning experiences through VR simulations, particularly valuable for fields like engineering, medicine, and scientific research.

- **Artificial Intelligence (AI) Tutors:** Integrating AI-powered tutors to offer personalized feedback and guidance throughout the learning journey.

- **Global Expansion:** Localizing content and expanding partnerships to support and empower women in STEM worldwide.

Beyond the previously mentioned features like VR Labs and AI tutors, the platform can expand its impact through collaboration with schools and universities as they can integrate the platform's resources into STEM curriculums, fostering early engagement and interest in STEM fields among girls. Partnering with companies in STEM fields can also create opportunities for platform users to gain valuable industry experience and mentorship from experienced professionals. The platform can leverage its growing community to advocate for policy changes that promote gender equality in STEM workplaces, such as parental leave policies and unconscious bias training programs.

8. Content Marketing Strategy: Spreading the Word and Reaching Your Audience

- Identifying Your Target Audience: Who are you trying to reach?

- Segmenting the audience: Women in STEM at different career stages (e.g., students, early-career professionals, senior leaders)
- Developing Compelling Content: Creating magnetic content to attract and engage.
  - Blog posts highlighting success stories and career advice
  - Social media campaigns featuring user-generated content and platform updates
  - Podcasts and webinars with industry leaders and role models
- Leveraging Social Media Platforms: Building a Community Online
  - Creating engaging communities on platforms like LinkedIn, Twitter, and Instagram
  - Partnering with STEM-focused influencers to reach a wider audience
- Search Engine Optimization (SEO): Making it easy for users to find you
  - Optimizing website content with relevant keywords
  - Building backlinks from high-authority websites in the STEM and women's empowerment space

9. Evaluation and Measurement: Tracking Progress and Impact

- Defining Key Performance Indicators (KPIs): How will you measure success?

- User engagement metrics (e.g., course completion rates, participation in discussions)
- Number of new members and content creators
- Career outcomes of platform users (e.g., promotions, job changes)
  - Conducting User Surveys: Gathering feedback for continuous improvement
    - Regularly soliciting feedback from users to understand their needs and preferences
  - Utilizing Data Analytics: Making data-driven decisions
    - Analyzing user data to identify areas for improvement and optimize the platform's effectiveness

The Spark Within: Rekindling a Passion for Physics

Rain lashed against the windowpane, mirroring the storm brewing inside Marie. Textbooks lay scattered across her desk, each equation a silent accusation. "Maybe physics isn't for me," she mumbled, staring at a half-completed problem set. Memories of her childhood, filled with constellations and dreams of becoming an astronaut, felt like a distant galaxy.

College had been a rude awakening. The once enthusiastic freshman, surrounded by a sea of unfamiliar faces in her introductory physics class, now felt like a lone island. Professor Thompson, a brilliant but intimidating man, seemed oblivious to her struggles. A discouraging comment from a peer about "girls not being cut out for this" echoed in her mind, chipping away at her confidence.

Disheartened, Marie contemplated changing her majors. Just then, a notification popped up on her laptop. It was from a new online platform called "**EmShe**." Intrigued, she clicked on it. A vibrant community unfolded before her eyes – women from diverse backgrounds, all united by their passion for science and technology. Success stories of accomplished female physicists, interactive coding challenges, and a forum filled with supportive discussions – it was everything Marie had been missing.

One profile, in particular, caught her eye. Dr. Evelyn Ramirez, a renowned astrophysicist, spoke of her struggles – feeling out of place and battling self-doubt. Yet, she persevered, fueled by a love for the cosmos. Marie saw a reflection of herself in Dr. Ramirez, a relatable role model shattering the myth of effortless genius.

Emboldened, Marie delved into the platform's resources. Interactive simulations brought complex concepts to life, gamified challenges made learning fun, and the supportive forum became her lifeline. Senior women in physics offered mentorship, patiently guiding her through challenging problems. Slowly, the spark within Marie reignited.

One evening, Marie posted on the forum, "I finally solved the blackbody radiation problem! Thanks to everyone for the encouragement." A flurry of responses followed, filled with congratulations and virtual high-fives. This sense of belonging, of being part of a sisterhood, was what Marie craved.

Empowered by her newfound confidence, Marie approached Professor Thompson during his office hours. Hesitantly at first, she explained her struggles and her newfound determination. To her surprise, Professor Thompson was receptive. He offered her additional guidance, recognizing the talent beneath her self-doubt.

Months later, Marie stood before the class, presenting a research paper on exoplanet atmospheres – a topic that once seemed daunting. Her voice trembled slightly at first, but as she spoke, her passion shone through. The same professor who once seemed unapproachable offered her a warm smile and a proud nod.

Marie's journey wasn't over. There would be more challenges and more moments of self-doubt. But now, she had a community behind her, a platform that had not just equipped her with skills but had rekindled the spark within. The little girl who dreamt of stars now had the tools and the confidence to reach for them. While the leaky pipeline might not be entirely plugged, Marie's story stands as a testament to the power of a supportive network and the unwavering spirit of a woman in STEM.

Conclusion: A Catalyst for Change - Empowering Women in STEM

The landscape of Science, Technology, Engineering, and Mathematics (STEM) is undeniably transformative. From groundbreaking discoveries that fuel medical advancements to technological innovations that shape the way we live and work, STEM fields hold immense potential to address some of humanity's most pressing challenges. However, this potential remains unrealized as long as women, who represent half the world's population, continue to be underrepresented in these critical sectors.

This chapter has explored the stark reality of the current situation. We've delved into the historical context, highlighting the struggles of pioneering women in STEM who paved the way for future generations. We've examined statistics that reveal the significant gender gap in various STEM disciplines. Furthermore, we've acknowledged the persistent challenges faced by women in STEM, including unconscious bias, lack of support systems, the gender pay gap, and the "leaky pipeline" phenomenon.

But this narrative doesn't have to end here. It's time to break down these barriers and create a more inclusive and equitable environment where women in STEM can thrive. The proposed platform, designed specifically to empower women in STEM, offers a beacon of hope. By fostering a comprehensive and supportive ecosystem, it can equip women with the skills, confidence, and connections they need to excel in their chosen fields.

Fostering a Supportive Community: Where Women Connect and Thrive

The platform doesn't just offer resources; it fosters a supportive community. Themed discussion forums allow women to connect with peers who share their unique experiences and challenges, fostering a sense of camaraderie and belonging. Mentorship circles offer personalized guidance and support, allowing women to learn from a diverse range of mentors and benefit from peer-to-peer connections.

Recognizing the unique pressures faced by women in STEM, the platform prioritizes mental well-being. It curates' resources promoting mental health, including guided meditations, yoga tutorials, and access to online therapy resources. Furthermore, a clear and comprehensive safe space policy ensures all users feel comfortable and respected when participating in discussions or online communities.

Celebrating achievements, big and small, is also crucial. A virtual recognition wall allows users to acknowledge each other's successes, fostering a sense of community and motivating users to keep pushing forward. Additionally, a dedicated blog section allows user-generated content. Here, women can share their personal stories, career journeys, and technical skills through articles, tutorials, or even creative projects. This not only empowers women to become leaders within the platform but also provides valuable and inspiring content for other users.

A Force for Change: Redefining the Landscape of STEM

The platform's success stories and profiles of accomplished women in STEM can serve as powerful inspiration for young girls considering STEM careers. This can help close the gender gap early on and create a pipeline of future female leaders in science and technology. By empowering more women to contribute their talents and expertise, the platform can accelerate progress towards a more equitable and sustainable future for all.

The Ripple Effect: Inspiring the Next Generation and Addressing Global Challenges

The impact of this platform extends far beyond its registered users. By fostering a thriving community of successful women in STEM, it becomes a powerful role model for young girls considering STEM careers. The platform's success stories, interactive features, and user-generated content showcasing diverse career paths can spark curiosity and ignite a passion for science and technology in the next generation. This can significantly close the gender gap early on, ensuring a future STEM workforce that is rich in talent and brimming with innovative ideas.

Furthermore, by empowering more women to enter and excel in STEM fields, the platform contributes to tackling some of the world's most pressing challenges.

Climate change, food security, and sustainable development are just a few areas that require solutions rooted in science, technology, engineering, and mathematics. When women are excluded from these fields, valuable perspectives and approaches are left untapped. By increasing the participation of women in STEM, the platform empowers them to contribute their unique talents and expertise to find solutions for a more equitable and sustainable future for all.

Building a Sustainable Future: Partnerships and Continuous Development

The platform's long-term success hinges on building strong partnerships and a commitment to continuous development. Collaborating with educational institutions can integrate the platform's resources into STEM curriculums, fostering early engagement and interest in these fields among girls. Partnering with companies in STEM fields can create internship and mentorship opportunities, providing valuable industry experience for platform users and fostering connections with experienced professionals.

Advocacy efforts can leverage the platform's growing community to push for policy changes that promote gender equality in STEM workplaces. This could include advocating for parental leave policies, unconscious bias training programs, and funding initiatives that support women in STEM research and development endeavors.

The platform's commitment to continuous development ensures it remains relevant and impactful. Future developments like incorporating Virtual Reality (VR) labs and Artificial Intelligence (AI) tutors can provide users with immersive learning experiences and personalized guidance throughout their STEM journeys. Additionally, global expansion efforts can localize content and establish partnerships to empower and support women in STEM worldwide.

A Call to Action: Join the Movement

The time for change is now. The potential for a future where women actively shape the landscape of STEM is within reach. This platform catalyzes positive change, but its success relies on a collective effort.

We invite women in STEM to join this movement. Here, you'll find the resources, support, and community you need to excel in your chosen field. Share your knowledge, experiences, and stories to inspire others. Let's build a platform that empowers women to shatter glass ceilings and reach their full potential.

We also call upon industry leaders, policymakers, educators, and allies to join us in this endeavor. Advocate for change, create inclusive workplaces, and mentor the next generation of women in STEM. By working together, we can unlock the immense potential of women in these critical fields and create a brighter future for all.

Let this platform be the spark that ignites a revolution in STEM. Let it be the space where women are not just encouraged to participate but empowered to lead. The future of science, technology, engineering, and mathematics is brimming with possibilities, and women are poised to play a pivotal role in shaping it. Join us, and together, let's redefine what's possible.

Chapter- 11

Pawsitive Match: Revolutionizing the Search for Your Furry (or Feathery) Friend

"Pawsitive Match" is an ingenious brand name that expertly melds "paws," the key feature of animals, and "positive," emphasizing the positive influence and advantage of locating one's ideal Emotional Support Animal. The moniker aptly summarizes this organization's objective to craft constructive matches between people and their four-legged (or winged) friends, promoting emotional stability and joy by nurturing cheerful relationships with them.

Introduction: The Power of the Human-Animal Bond

The connection between humans and animals is transformative, offering emotional and mental health benefits that cannot be understated. Research consistently shows that interacting with animals can reduce stress, alleviate symptoms of anxiety and depression, and provide a sense of comfort. Emotional Support Animals (ESAs) are becoming more popular as people seek companionship that offer essential emotional support.

However, finding the right ESA can be a challenging experience. Much like online dating, it requires careful consideration of personal needs, lifestyle factors, and environmental constraints. Traditional avenues, such as animal shelters or classified listings, often focus solely on breed or appearance, leaving individuals uncertain about whether the chosen animal will meet their emotional and lifestyle requirements.

Pawsitive Match: Your Path to Emotional Well-Being

This is where **Pawsitive Match** steps in. Pawsitive Match harnesses the power of Artificial Intelligence (AI) to make the process of finding the perfect ESA more accessible and tailored to individual needs. Through an intuitive platform, users are guided step-by-step to discover their ideal companion, ensuring a personalized experience that prioritizes emotional well-being.

Beyond Finding a Pet: Understanding the Key Challenges

Selecting the right ESA goes beyond simply picking a breed or species. Individuals face several obstacles when searching for a suitable companion:

- **Identifying the Right Animal**: Determining which species or breed will align with a person's unique needs and lifestyle can be tricky. Factors such as living in a small space or dealing with allergies need to be considered carefully. For example, a high-energy dog breed may not be ideal for someone with limited outdoor space, while finding a hypoallergenic animal that also meets emotional support requirements may prove difficult.

- **Care and Training**: The responsibilities of owning an ESA extend to understanding their care needs, from dietary restrictions to exercise and training requirements. The challenge of ensuring the animal is properly trained to provide specific emotional support can be overwhelming without proper guidance.

- **Access to Professional Guidance**: Many individuals have limited access to experts like therapists or animal behaviorists who specialize in ESA selection and care. The involvement of both mental health professionals and animal experts is crucial to ensure the animal's suitability and smooth integration into an individual's lifestyle. However, finding professionals with this expertise can be both time-consuming and costly.

Pawsitive Match: A Holistic Solution

Pawsitive Match offers a comprehensive solution to these challenges, ensuring users are supported every step of the way:

- **Personalized Matching**: Using AI-driven technology, Pawsitive Match provides a questionnaire to assess an individual's lifestyle, needs, and potential allergens. Based on the responses, the platform recommends suitable ESA options, ensuring compatibility in both temperament and care requirements.

- **Educational Resources**: Users have access to a wealth of knowledge on ESA care, training, and responsible pet ownership. Pawsitive Match's library includes guides written by veterinary experts and animal behaviorists, covering topics from grooming and dietary needs to managing common behavioral challenges.

- **Expert Consultations**: The platform connects users with licensed therapists and animal behaviorists for personalized advice. Whether through chat, phone calls, or video sessions, users can seek expert guidance to ensure their ESA is the right fit for their emotional needs and lifestyle.

Beyond the App: Extending the Support System

Pawsitive Match extends its services beyond the app, offering additional resources and fostering a supportive community for ESA owners:

- **Consultations with Professionals**: Users can choose from in-app consultations, phone calls, or in-person meetings with qualified therapists and animal behaviorists. This flexibility ensures that users can access the guidance they need in a way that suits them best.

- **Blog and Webinars**: The platform regularly updates its blog with articles from mental health experts, animal trainers, and veterinarians, offering insights into ESA care, training, and the science behind the human-animal bond. Webinars provide real-time learning opportunities, while a secure online community connects users to share experiences and advice.

- **Partnerships with Shelters**: By collaborating with shelters across the country, Pawsitive Match promotes the adoption of shelter animals as ESAs, ensuring they undergo proper health and behavioral assessments before being recommended to new owners.

Unique Selling Propositions of Pawsitive Match

Pawsitive Match distinguishes itself through several key features:

- **AI-Powered Compatibility**: Unlike traditional adoption methods, the platform uses sophisticated AI to match users with the most compatible ESAs, leading to stronger, longer-lasting human-animal bonds.

- **Focus on Responsible Adoption**: By partnering with shelters, Pawsitive Match ensures that animals are responsibly adopted and matched to individuals who can meet their needs.

- **Comprehensive Support**: Beyond matching, Pawsitive Match provides a robust support system that includes expert consultations, educational resources, and a community forum for ongoing assistance.

- **Commitment to Research**: In collaboration with universities and research institutions, Pawsitive Match actively contributes to the study of human-animal interactions, ensuring that their services remain cutting-edge.

A Journey to Unconditional Love

Pawsitive Match isn't just an app; it's a catalyst for a transformative relationship. It bridges the gap between you and an ESA, providing not just a furry (or feathery) confidante, but also a source of unwavering support, and a spark of joy in your daily life.

Imagine the weight of anxiety lifting as you cuddle with your perfectly matched ESA, a gentle Golden Retriever whose calming presence brings a sense of peace. Picture the loneliness dissolving as you share laughter and playful moments during your daily walks with your loyal companion. Pawsitive Match unlocks these possibilities, tailoring the journey to your specific needs and fostering a bond that transcends the label of "emotional support."

Pawsitive Blog & Webinars: Example Topics

Pawsitive Blog:

- **Understanding ESAs:** This blog series could cover the legalities and qualifications for ESAs, different types of emotional support animals (dogs, cats, even miniature horses!), and navigating conversations with landlords or employers.
- **Building a Bond with Your ESA:** Articles could delve into creating a training routine, understanding animal communication cues, fostering trust and attachment, and addressing common behavioral challenges.

- **Living with an ESA:** This series could offer tips on creating a pet-friendly home environment, managing pet care costs on a budget, finding pet-friendly travel options, and incorporating your ESA into your daily routine.

- **Mental Health and Animal Companionship:** Blog posts could explore the science behind the human-animal bond, the benefits of ESAs for specific mental health conditions (anxiety, depression, PTSD), and success stories from Pawsitive Match users.

- **Species Spotlight:** This series could introduce different animal companions suitable as ESAs, delve into their unique needs and temperaments (rabbits, guinea pigs, birds), and offer breed-specific training and care recommendations.

Pawsitive Webinars:

- **Choosing the Right ESA for You:** Live webinars hosted by veterinarians, animal behaviorists, and Pawsitive Match therapists could guide users through the matching process, considering lifestyle factors, allergies, and emotional needs.

- **Train Your ESA Like a Pro:** A series of interactive webinars could demonstrate basic and advanced training techniques for various animal companions, featuring professional dog trainers or animal behaviorists.

- **Ask the Experts:** Live Q&A sessions with Pawsitive Match's network of licensed therapists and animal behaviorists could address user concerns about integrating an ESA into their lives, managing behavioral issues, or navigating mental health challenges.

- **Desensitization and Counterconditioning Techniques for ESAs:** Webinars could delve into specific strategies for addressing common ESA anxieties, like separation anxiety or fear of loud noises, using positive reinforcement methods.

- **Travelling with Your ESA:** Live sessions could provide tips on navigating airline pet policies, finding pet-friendly accommodations, and ensuring a smooth travel experience for you and your furry friend.

These are just a few examples, and the Pawsitive Match blog and webinars can cover a wide range of topics to keep users informed, engaged, and supported throughout their ESA journey.

From Rain to Rainbows: How Pawsitive Match Helped Amelia Find Hope (and a Furry Friend)

Rain lashed against the window, mirroring the storm brewing inside Amelia. The once vibrant colors of her apartment seemed muted and the silence felt deafening. Loneliness, a constant companion these past few months, tightened its cold grip on her heart. Medication helped, but it couldn't fill the void left by the loss of her beloved dog, Charlie.

Charlie, a scruffy terrier mix with a heart as big as his ears, had been Amelia's anchor for ten years. He'd witnessed her triumphs and held her paw (well, licked her tears) through every heartbreak. After a sudden illness took him, Amelia felt adrift, the world a bleak landscape.

One gloomy afternoon, a friend mentioned Pawsitive Match. Skeptical at first, Amelia downloaded the app with a sigh. The initial questions felt intrusive, but as she answered, a sliver of hope flickered. The app delved deeper than just breed preferences, probing her anxieties and emotional needs.

Days later, a notification popped up – "Your Purrfect Match Awaits!" Amelia's heart hammered as she opened the profile. There, staring back with emerald eyes, was Oliver, a ginger tabby with a mischievous glint. His bio, written in a playful voice, mentioned a love for napping in sunbeams and chasing dust bunnies (with questionable success).

Amelia felt a hesitant smile tug at her lips. Could this quirky cat be the answer?

At the shelter, a nervous energy crackled in the air. Then, a volunteer brought out a ginger blur who promptly darted under a chair. Suddenly, Oliver peeked out, his eyes wide and curious.

Amelia knelt, extending a tentative hand. Oliver sniffed it cautiously, then nudged it with his head. A purr rumbled in his tiny chest as he rubbed against her leg.

Tears welled up in Amelia's eyes, not of sadness this time, but of a tentative hope. Walking out of the shelter with Oliver nestled in a carrier, she felt a lightness she hadn't experienced in months.

Life wasn't perfect - Oliver had a knack for knocking things off shelves with laser focus - but he brought laughter and a sense of purpose back into Amelia's life. His comforting presence chased away the shadows of loneliness, reminding her that love, like a purr, can come in the most unexpected forms.

Pawsitive Match hadn't just connected her with an ESA, it had reconnected her with a piece of herself, the part that believed in joy, companionship, and the unconditional love only a furry friend can offer.

A Second Chance at Adventure: Max and Ben

Max, a golden retriever with a perpetually wagging tail, hadn't always been the picture of canine contentment. Abandoned as a puppy, he bounced from foster home to foster home, his playful spirit dampened by confusion and a yearning for a place to call his own. Ben, a retired firefighter, found himself in a similar situation. After a knee injury forced him into early retirement, the once active, social man felt isolated and adrift.

Their paths crossed at a local shelter hosting a Pawsitive Match adoption event. Ben, hesitant at first, was drawn to Max's goofy grin and playful energy. Max, sensing a kindred spirit, showered Ben with enthusiastic slobbery kisses. It was an instant connection.

The Pawsitive Match app confirmed what their hearts already knew. Ben's calm demeanor perfectly balanced Max's boundless enthusiasm. More importantly, the app's resources helped Ben understand Max's past and provided him with training tips to address any lingering anxieties.

Their days took on a new rhythm. Ben, no longer confined by his injury, rediscovered the joy of walks in the park, Max by his side, a furry shadow of pure happiness. They explored new trails, the wind whipping through their fur and hair. Max's playful nudges coaxed Ben out of his shell, encouraging him to reconnect with old friends and neighbors.

One afternoon, while exploring a new path, Ben stumbled, his knee buckling beneath him. Pain shot through his leg, and a wave of despair threatened to engulf him. Before he could even whimper, Max was beside him, whining softly and nudging him with his wet nose. Ben wrapped his arm around Max's furry neck, drawing comfort from his warmth and unwavering presence.

Using his training from Pawsitive Match, Ben managed to call for help. As they waited for the ambulance, Max never left his side, a silent, loyal companion. In the hospital, Ben learned he needed surgery, but the worry was tempered by the knowledge that he wouldn't face it alone.

Max became a regular visitor at the hospital, his happy bark a beacon of hope in the sterile environment. He brought smiles to the faces of other patients and staff alike, a furry ambassador of unconditional love.

With time and physical therapy, Ben recovered. He never fully regained the use of his knee, but that didn't stop him and Max. They traded long hikes for shorter, scenic walks, enjoying the simple pleasure of companionship. Max became Ben's therapy dog, visiting schools and senior centers, and spreading joy wherever they went.

Pawsitive Match wasn't just about finding an ESA; it was about rekindling a love for life. For Max, it was a loving home, a second chance at adventure. For Ben, it was a furry companion who reminded him of his strength and resilience, a loyal friend who walked beside him, every step of the way.

Conclusion: Pawsitive Connections for a Brighter Future

The stories of Amelia and Ben are just a glimpse into the profound impact Pawsitive Match can have on lives. We create more than just matches; we foster connections that provide emotional support, unconditional love, and a renewed sense of purpose.

Pawsitive Match goes beyond matchmaking. We cultivate a supportive community dedicated to responsible pet ownership and the human-animal bond. By leveraging technology and scientific research, we strive to create a brighter future for both individuals and animals. But our journey doesn't stop here. We are committed to continuous improvement, constantly seeking ways to refine our matching algorithm, enhance the user experience, and expand our community features to provide even more support.

Join us on this journey. Together, let's unlock the power of positive connections and build a world where everyone has a furry (or feathery) friend by their side. Download the Pawsitive Match app today to start your personalized journey towards emotional well-being with an ESA companion. Visit our website to learn more about Pawsitive Match, our commitment to responsible pet ownership, and the science behind the human-animal bond.

Share your own stories of animal companionship on social media.

Let's create a ripple effect of pawsitivity together!"

Chapter-12

Freshen Up: Cleanliness. Convenience. Comfort.

The principles behind "Freshen Up" are reflected in its name, which symbolizes cleanliness, convenience, and comfort. By employing the term "freshen," users can anticipate being revitalized after a tiring journey by experiencing rejuvenation and hygiene when utilizing the facilities provided. The word "up" conveys not only the idea of improved personal sanitation but also highlights the ease of finding accessible restrooms and showers. "Freshen Up" combines a seamless and effortless way to access hygienic and comfortable amenities, making it an ideal choice for busy travelers and commuters in need of a fast revitalization.

Hygiene stands as one of the paramount concerns for anyone, irrespective of their background. Yet, the simple act of finding a restroom in public settings is often overlooked. Unfortunately, many public restrooms suffer from poor hygiene and limited accessibility.

In numerous cities, visitors, tourists, and urban residents face the challenge of limited access to clean and convenient restrooms. This not only impacts their health and dignity but also poses significant environmental and social risks. Addressing this issue effectively requires innovative solutions, such as the introduction of portable toilets that are easy to install, maintain, and relocate.

Now, you might ask: how are these portable toilets managed? Will they end up as unhygienic as conventional public restrooms? Well, portable toilets are specifically engineered to be compact, lightweight, and durable. They feature self-contained waste management systems designed to minimize odors and contamination. These toilets can be deployed across various locations such as parks, markets, slums, and festivals, where traditional sanitation facilities are inadequate or unavailable.

The deployment of portable toilets offers multiple benefits to both users and society at large. They provide a safe, comfortable, and accessible option for individuals to relieve themselves, particularly benefiting vulnerable groups like women, children, and the elderly who are more susceptible to harassment and infections.

Let's explore a few real-world scenarios where restroom availability has become a pressing issue. By examining each case, we can better understand the urgency and the necessity for innovative startup ideas like "Freshen Up."

Case 1: Aspiring UPSC Candidate

Amit, an aspiring UPSC candidate from Patna, is in Delhi for an interview. He arrived at 8 am with his interview scheduled for 11 am. With only 3 hours to spare, finding clean and available restrooms at the bus stands and railway stations is a mammoth task. He cannot afford a decent Hotel or guest house.

This is a common problem faced by many travelers and commuters in Delhi, especially those arriving from other cities or states for work or education purposes. According to a report, 3.4 million travelers visited Delhi in 2019 pre-COVID. However, the availability and quality of public restrooms in the city are inadequate and unsatisfactory.

Case 2: A Tourist from Finland

Amanda, a solo tourist from Finland, loves exploring historical monuments and UNESCO heritage sites. During her visit to Ahmedabad, a city in India, known for its rich cultural and architectural heritage. She wants to visit the famous Sabarmati Ashram, the Adalaj Stepwell, the Jama Masjid, the Sarkhej Roza, and of course, the world's biggest cricket stadium in Ahmedabad city.

However, Amanda faces a common challenge encountered by female travelers in India: finding safe and hygienic restrooms. She does not want to hire a hotel room for a full day as she is on a budget and prefers to travel light. Concerns about security and hygiene heighten her apprehension.

She wishes there was a solution that could provide her with a clean, comfortable and secure place to use the toilet, and freshen up while she enjoys the sights of the city. She wonders if there is such a thing as a portable restroom that can be installed at strategic locations near tourist attractions and public places.

Case 3: A Devotee of Sri Venkateshwara Temple

Subramanyam Swami, a devotee of Sri Venkateshwara temple in the hill town of Tirumala at Tirupati, Andhra Pradesh embarks on his one-day visit to the holy shrine. After hours of waiting in the queue to get a glimpse of the deity and offer his prayers, he urgently needs to use a restroom. Reluctant to leave the queue, he looks around and sees that the nearest public restroom is overcrowded.

He wishes there was a better solution for this common challenge faced by many pilgrims. He thinks that portable restrooms are a good startup idea that can cater to the needs of the devotees. He imagines how convenient it would be to have a clean and comfortable restroom that can be easily moved and installed at different locations. Swami hopes that someone will take up this initiative and make his next visit to the temple more pleasant and satisfying.

Case 4: A Candidate with An MBA Postgraduate Degree in Finance

Shreya, an MBA postgraduate in Finance, travels to Mumbai for a crucial interview with a fintech company in Bandra. She only has a few hours to spend in the city before she has to catch a train back to her hometown in Uttarakhand at 6 pm.

However, she confronts a common issue faced by travelers in India: the lack of clean and safe public restrooms. Reluctant to use the crowded and unsanitary toilets at the railway station or roadside stalls, she seeks alternatives that uphold her dignity and hygiene.

Case 5: An Urban Poor Individual Who Lives in Slums

Munna is one of the millions of urban poor who live in the slums in Mumbai, the financial capital of India. He faces many challenges in his daily life, among the most pressing is the lack of access to adequate sanitation facilities. Sharing a public toilet with hundreds of residents proves inconvenient, unsanitary, and sometimes unsafe.

He has to wake up before dawn to avoid long queues and confrontations with other users, who sometimes fight over the limited space and water. Munna dreams of having a home with a dedicated toilet, but in a city where real estate prices are sky high and affordable housing remains scarce, this dream seems far from achievable.

The Startup Idea Projection 1: Common Solution

Freshen Up proposes an integrated restroom solution for travelers and residents, offering convenient, hygienic, and accessible facilities. This initiative involves strategically positioned portable restrooms, supported by a mobile app, that offers additional services to cater to diverse restroom needs.

Portable Restrooms:

Freshen Up plans to install portable restrooms in key locations across the country, addressing the city's lack of public restroom facilities. These units will be equipped with toilets, sinks, mirrors, fans, lights, and locks. They can be connected to water and sewage systems or utilize self-contained tanks.

Some units will be equipped with solar panels, Wi-Fi, CCTV cameras, and GPS tracking for enhanced functionality and security. These portable restrooms will provide a more hygienic and stress-free restroom experience for both travelers and residents.

Improved Restrooms for Women

The portable restrooms are not only beneficial for tourists but also for residents, particularly women facing sanitation challenges. Some cities and small towns struggle with open defecation issues and making Freshen Up's portable restrooms can help address these concerns by providing safe and private facilities for women. The strategically placed restrooms will be designed with women's safety and comfort in mind, providing a much-needed amenity for them.

The Freshen Up mobile app called "**Freshen Up**" can be downloaded on smartphones through the App Store or Google Play. The app will empower users to locate nearby, well-maintained restrooms verified and rated by other users, ensuring a hygienic and pleasant experience.

Tentative app name: Freshen Up

User input data: After entering basic credentials, the user selects their location and the desired service (shower or restroom).

Output:

- Display of availability of facilities.
- Information on time and distance required to reach the chosen destination.
- Display of pricing per cabin.

App Features:

- **Restroom Locator:** The app uses GPS to identify nearby restrooms, including strategically placed portable units and partner facilities.

- **Amenities and Ratings:** Users can view the amenities offered such as showers, toiletries, cleanliness, and accessibility alongside user ratings and reviews.

- **Real-time Availability:** Users will receive up-to-date information on restroom availability to avoid unnecessary searches and long waiting times.

- **In-App Payment:** Freshen Up will offer in-app payment options for a seamless and cashless restroom experience.

- **Security and Safety:** Restroom locations will be carefully selected for safety, and the app will have security features such as CCTV surveillance to ensure user safety.

To further enhance the restroom experience, Freshen Up will collaborate with selected partners to offer supplementary amenities such as temporary luggage storage, refreshment stations, and device charging facilities at select locations.

Locations:

Airports, railway stations, bus depots, religious centres, colleges, and hospitals.

Imagine travelling to a new city for a business meeting. After a long flight, you arrive at the airport and need to freshen up before heading to the office. Finding a hotel or a public restroom is time-consuming and inconvenient. What do you do?

You pull out your phone and open the Freshen Up app. This app helps you find the nearest facility where you can take a shower or use a restroom. You select your current location (airport) and choose the required service. The app instantly displays the availability of cabins, the time and distance required to reach them, along with the pricing per cabin. You can also view ratings and reviews from other users.

You pick a cabin close to your terminal with good reviews. Using your credit card, you can make the payment and receive a confirmation code. The app provides directions, and within minutes, you arrive at the cabin. Upon entering the code, you step inside a clean, spacious cabin equipped with towels, toiletries, and a hairdryer. You enjoy a refreshing shower and get ready for your meeting.

Once you exit the cabin, you rate your experience on the app and receive a payment receipt. Feeling confident and energized, you head to the office, grateful to Freshen Up for making your trip more comfortable and convenient.

The Startup Idea Projection 2: Social Solution

Freshen Up aims to create a sustainable and inclusive restroom solution for the residents, particularly those in slum areas, by expanding community toilet facilities. This initiative involves cooperation between municipal authorities, civil society organizations, and the local community to ensure effective implementation and maintenance of the facilities.

The project will commence by identifying densely populated areas, especially in the slums, where the existing restroom facilities are limited or inadequate. Detailed surveys and consultations with the local community will be conducted to understand their specific needs and preferences.

Based on the findings, well-designed community toilet complexes will be constructed, ensuring they are easily accessible to residents. The complexes will include separate sections for men, women, and persons with disabilities, each equipped with clean, well-maintained toilets, washbasins, and hygiene amenities.

To ensure the long-term sustainability and hygiene of the community toilets, the Empowered Sanitation Initiative will engage the local community in facility management. Training and employment opportunities will be provided to members of the community, enabling them to oversee and operate the facilities.

A community-based maintenance team will be formed to ensure regular cleaning, supply restocking, and prompt resolution of maintenance issues. Regular health and hygiene awareness campaigns will also be conducted to promote responsible restroom usage and cleanliness.

Revenue Model:

Revenue is generated through cabin usage fees, which vary based on the duration of usage (e.g., 10, 15, or 20 minutes) and service type (shower or restroom).

Cabin Usage Fees:

CABIN	10 MIN	15 MIN	20 MIN
SHOWER	50	75	100
TOILET	10	30	50

Advertising:

The trailer's exterior will provide prime advertising space for brands seeking to reach a wide and diverse audience. Sponsors can partner with Freshen Up to display advertisements on the top or back of the trailer, generating additional revenue while promoting their products or services.

Freshen Up envisions introducing a mobile restroom solution through state-of-the-art truck trailers. Its meticulously designed features, focus on hygiene, and commitment to user convenience will make it a must-have service for travelers and commuters seeking a seamless restroom experience. The adaptable and sustainable revenue model, combined with innovative design and functionality.

Design, Dimensions, and Structure

The Freshen Up truck trailer will be designed to optimize space and portability. Its dimensions will be carefully planned to ensure it can easily fit into various parking spaces and public areas across different locations. The exterior will feature captivating branding, including the Freshen Up logo and eye-catching designs that draw attention and inform passersby about the service.

Functionality and Features:

The trailer will be equipped with an array of features to provide users with a comfortable and convenient restroom experience:

Restroom Cabins: The trailer will house multiple private cabins, specifically designed for men and women. The number of cabins will be thoughtfully determined based on the trailer's size and capacity.

Shower Facilities: Some versions of the Freshen Up trailer will have an upper deck for shower cabins, equipped with water heaters, high-quality toiletries, and soft towels for a refreshing and rejuvenating experience.

Hygiene and Sanitation: Ensuring the highest standard of cleanliness, the trailer will implement a rigorous cleaning and sanitization routine and a sophisticated waste management system for proper disposal and maintenance of waste and sewage.

Storage Space: Users will have access to secure temporary storage options to store their belongings while they use the facilities.

Accessibility and Safety: The trailer will prioritize accessibility, incorporating ramps, handrails, and other features to cater to individuals with mobility challenges. Additionally, security will be enhanced with CCTV cameras and real-time monitoring.

Energy Efficiency: Demonstrating its commitment to sustainability, Freshen Up will be equipped with energy-efficient features, including solar panels, to minimize its environmental impact and operational costs.

Gaining Traction for Freshen Up

User-Centric Approach: Freshen Up will focus on providing a seamless user experience. Word-of-mouth referrals and positive reviews from satisfied users will be essential in attracting new customers.

Marketing Campaigns: Implementing targeted online and offline marketing campaigns, to reach potential users and raise awareness about the app. Social media platforms, influencer partnerships, and local events can be effective channels.

Partnerships and Collaborations: Collaborate with travel portals, sightseeing agencies, hotels, restaurants, and public transportation companies to integrate Freshen Up into their services. This way, users will be encouraged to download and use the app during their travels.

Incentives for Users: Offer rewards and incentives for users who refer others to the app or share their restroom experiences, creating a viral loop and attracting more users.

Localized Expansion: Start by targeting specific cities or regions with a higher demand for clean restrooms. Once established, expand to other locations to create a larger user base.

Data-Driven Changes: Utilize user data and feedback to continuously improve app features and overall user experience.

A Win-Win Situation for The Stakeholders Sponsor Involvement and Business

Sponsors play a crucial role in monitoring and assessing the impact and performance of the Freshen Up project. By receiving regular reports and feedback from the service providers and users, sponsors gain valuable insights into the effectiveness of the initiative. Key metrics such as the number of users served, customer satisfaction ratings, and improvements in sanitation conditions in target areas provide a comprehensive understanding of the project's social impact and return on investment.

Value Proposition for Stakeholders

1. Benefits Provided to the Urban Poor

Freshen Up offers a compelling value proposition for all stakeholders, particularly the urban poor, who benefit immensely from gaining access to quality sanitation services. For individuals like Munna, who lives in a Mumbai slum, access to clean and safe restroom facilities can significantly enhance daily life. Hygienic toilets promote better health, dignity, and overall well-being. By providing these essential services, Freshen Up can help uplift marginalized communities and contribute to breaking the cycle of poverty.

2. Benefit for Municipal Corporations

Municipal corporations that own and operate Freshen Up trailers benefit in multiple ways:

- **Revenue generation:** The project's financial model relies on affordable cabin usage fees, ensuring services remain accessible to a broad audience, including those with limited financial means. This revenue can then be reinvested to maintain and expand the project, increasing its reach and impact.

- **Social Responsibility and Recognition:** By addressing the sanitation needs of the urban poor, municipal corporations demonstrate their commitment to community well-being and progress. Such initiatives can bolster their reputation and build trust with citizens in their local authorities, leading to increased public support and cooperation in other development projects.

3. Creating Opportunities for Sponsors

Sponsors who support the Freshen Up project gain publicity and recognition for their social contributions. Displaying advertisements on the top or back side of the trailers provides an opportunity to reach a large and diverse audience. These advertisements not only generate revenue but also showcase sponsors' commitment to social causes. Aligning their businesses with initiatives that improve the lives of marginalized communities can enhance their reputation and attract socially conscious consumers.

Ensuring Viability and Success

1. Collaboration and Partnerships

To ensure the viability and success of the Freshen Up project, effective collaboration and partnerships are essential. Municipal corporations must work closely with civil society organizations, NGOs, and local communities to identify suitable locations for trailer parking. Engaging with the target population helps understand their specific needs and preferences, allowing for continuous service improvement.

2. Protocols for Sanitation and Maintenance

High standards of cleanliness and hygiene are critical for the project's success. Regular cleaning of restroom cabins, proper waste management, and adherence to safety regulations must be established. Continuous monitoring and gathering of user feedback are necessary to identify the areas for improvement and address issues promptly.

- **Public Awareness and Acceptance**

Public awareness and acceptance are crucial for Freshen Up's success. Extensive marketing and outreach campaigns should inform the public about the availability and benefits of the services. Collaborations with local community leaders, educational institutions, and healthcare facilities can help spread the word and build trust among potential users. Leveraging digital platforms and social media will enhance visibility and reach a broader audience.

Conclusion

The Freshen Up project presents a viable and impactful solution to address the critical issue of sanitation access for the urban poor. By utilizing portable trailer trucks equipped with clean and well-maintained restroom cabins, the project aims to improve the health, dignity, and overall quality of life for marginalized communities.

Revenue generated from cabin usage fees and advertisements ensures a sustainable financial model and attracting sponsors who value social responsibility.

With careful planning, robust partnerships, and continuous monitoring, Freshen Up has the potential to make a significant positive impact on millions of lives, contributing to a more inclusive and sanitary urban environment.

Chapter-13

EcoValence: Nurturing a Sustainable Tomorrow

"Our dedication to promoting ecology and sustainability is embodied in the name EcoValence. It symbolizes fostering harmonious, sustainable practices within communities and institutions by utilizing "Eco" for ecological emphasis and "Valence" for dynamic interactions. This paves the way towards a prosperous future where the balance between humans and nature endures."

In the bustling metropolis of Delhi, the story of EcoValence's transformative impact unfolds against the backdrop of diverse neighborhoods, thriving business hubs, industrious districts, and the ever-active local government offices.

Let's journey with Namita, a determined resident of the leafy neighborhood of Vasant Kunj. Engrossed in EcoValence's carbon footprint tracker, Namita's passion for environmental change propels her to delve into her community's ecological impact. With every click and input, Namita's journey towards environmental enlightenment gains momentum. The tracker becomes her digital compass, guiding her through the intricacies of her community's ecological footprint.

Driven by her unwavering dedication to understanding and mitigating the environmental footprint of her locality, Namita meticulously navigates through the tracker's functionalities. She diligently enters data, creating a comprehensive picture of transportation habits, energy consumption patterns, waste management practices, and operational activities within her neighborhood.

As Namita delves deeper into the insights provided by EcoValence, a newfound understanding of her community's ecological imprint takes shape. She realizes the significance of collective action and the transformative power it holds in shaping a sustainable future. She tirelessly advocates for eco-conscious practices, rallying neighbors, local organizations, and authorities to join her in this environmental crusade. Her passion ignites a spark, drawing like-minded individuals together, united by a common goal— creating a greener and more sustainable Vasant Kunj.

Businesses in Nehru Place

Meanwhile, businesses operating within Nehru Place's commercial district integrate eco-friendly practices into their operations. These could include measures like switching to renewable energy sources, implementing energy-efficient technologies, reducing waste generation, optimizing transportation, or employing sustainable production methods.

EcoValence's carbon credit tracker monitors and quantifies the reduction in greenhouse gas emissions resulting from these eco-friendly practices. It collects data on the emission reductions achieved by the businesses. The emission reductions achieved are verified by recognized third-party certifiers. These certifiers authenticate the accuracy of the emission reduction claims made by the businesses. Verification involves rigorous assessments and audits to ensure compliance with international standards.

Upon successful verification, the businesses are awarded carbon credits equivalent to the volume of reduced emissions. Each credit typically represents one ton of carbon dioxide or its equivalent reduced or removed from the atmosphere. These credits are then added to the businesses' accounts. Businesses can utilize these earned carbon credits to offset their emissions or trade them on carbon markets. When they engage in emission-reducing activities, they can use these credits to compensate for a portion or the entirety of their remaining emissions, contributing to their sustainability goals.

Industrial Transformation in Okhla and Mayapuri

In the bustling industrial enclaves of Okhla and Mayapuri, industry leaders like Arjun are spearheading change. Leveraging EcoValence's suite of tools, Arjun engineers a radical transformation within his factory. Through meticulous energy optimization and strategic waste management, his facility significantly reduces its carbon footprint, earning notable carbon credits in the process.

Hand in hand, the local government, utilizing EcoValence's insights, propels industrial sectors towards sustainable technologies and practices.

Government Collaboration

In the intricate web of Delhi's administrative corridors, the local government has embraced EcoValence's innovative tools as indispensable assets for tracking, analyzing, and implementing environmental strategies across the city. The officials diligently pore over EcoValence's comprehensive reports, meticulously analyzing the detailed data the platform provides. This data serves as a powerful instrument, offering precise insights into various sectors' environmental impacts. By leveraging the analytics from the app, these officials discern trends, identify high-emission areas, and pinpoint zones requiring immediate environmental intervention.

Simultaneously, the collaborative efforts between the local government and EcoValence extend beyond data analysis. This synergy is a driving force behind shaping the government's environmental strategies, notably within industrial hubs like Okhla and Mayapuri. The carbon footprint and credit trackers play pivotal roles in enabling officials to monitor, incentivize, and reward sustainable practices undertaken by businesses, industries, and communities. Utilizing this information, the government formulates policies that encourage eco-friendly practices, providing incentives and recognition for impactful sustainability initiatives.

The government's utilization of EcoValence's tools goes beyond data collection; it extends to proactive engagement. Officials collaborate directly with communities, industries, and businesses, actively guiding and encouraging these stakeholders to adopt sustainable practices. By sharing insights from the app, providing resources, and fostering collaborative initiatives, they work towards fostering a culture of environmental responsibility.

Ultimately, the local government's embrace of EcoValence's suite of tools transcends mere tracking; it encompasses employing data-driven strategies, fostering collaboration, and catalyzing a city-wide movement towards a greener, more sustainable Delhi. Through this partnership, EcoValence stands as a crucial ally in the government's pursuit of a more environmentally conscious cityscape, driving change not only within industrial zones but throughout the fabric of Delhi's diverse landscape.

Addressing Today's Environmental Challenges

In today's world, an array of pressing environmental challenges demands our immediate attention, presenting a tapestry of interconnected issues that require a united response.

The delicate ecological balance, vital for our planet's sustenance, faces continuous threats from human-driven disruptions. Activities such as deforestation, habitat destruction, pollution, and rampant exploitation of natural resources jeopardize biodiversity and destabilize critical ecological processes. The risk of irreversible harm to ecosystems looms large, potentially triggering far-reaching environmental consequences, affecting both human societies and the overall health of our planet.

Venturing into the depths of our oceans reveals a silent but menacing crisis: ocean acidification. The oceans' increased absorption of carbon dioxide induces chemical changes, endangering marine life, particularly those reliant on calcium carbonate shells like corals and shellfish. This phenomenon poses severe threats to marine ecosystems, fisheries, and the broader spectrum of biodiversity.

Yet, amidst these challenges, environmental inequality casts a dark shadow. Marginalized communities, often due to social, economic, and geographical disparities, bear the disproportionate burden of environmental hazards. Lacking access to clean resources and proper infrastructure, these communities become highly susceptible to the adverse impacts of pollution, climate change, and environmental degradation.

Globalization, while fostering economic interconnectivity, amplifies environmental pressures. The expansive global supply chains drive heightened resource extraction, increased emissions from manufacturing, and the sprawl of extensive transportation networks. This intricate web of interconnectedness magnifies environmental footprints, necessitating a rethinking of global trade practices for a more sustainable future.

Navigating these challenges encounters significant obstacles in policy-making realms. The implementation of stringent environmental policies faces hurdles stemming from complex political, economic, and social factors. The struggle to reconcile conflicting interests and enforce effective global initiatives poses a formidable challenge, requiring a delicate balance between economic development and environmental preservation on a global scale.

To steer toward sustainability, education and behavioral shifts are pivotal. Raising awareness, promoting responsible consumption patterns, and nurturing eco-conscious mindsets play an instrumental role in driving systemic changes in societal norms and individual actions. Education empowers individuals and communities to make informed decisions contributing positively to environmental welfare.

Tackling these multifaceted challenges necessitates collaborative efforts, innovative solutions, adaptive policies, and unwavering commitment from global stakeholders. A comprehensive approach acknowledging the intricate complexity while striving for a sustainable and resilient future for both humanity and the planet is indispensable.

Addressing these intricate and interconnected challenges demands collaborative efforts, innovative solutions, adaptive policies, and a resolute commitment from global stakeholders. It requires a holistic approach that acknowledges the complexity of these issues while striving for a sustainable and resilient future for both humanity and the planet.

Unique Selling Point (USP) of EcoValence

EcoValence stands as a visionary mobile application meticulously tailored to empower communities, local governments, large-scale industries, offices, and educational institutions within specific geographical areas spanning a minimum of 10 km². In an era marked by pressing environmental challenges, this app emerges as a beacon, offering tailored solutions and a unified path towards harmonious, sustainable living within defined localities.

- **Tailored Environmental Assessment**

EcoValence features an adaptive carbon footprint calculator specifically designed for communities, industries, offices, and educational institutions within the 10 to 1500 km² region. Users can input area-specific data on transportation, energy consumption, waste generation, and operational practices to reveal collective environmental impact. This precise assessment enables each locality to understand its unique environmental footprint, setting the foundation for targeted sustainability measures.

- **Customized Sustainability Roadmaps**

The app crafts tailored sustainability roadmaps advocating area-specific strategies such as energy efficiency, sustainable transportation, waste management, and initiatives for local governance, industries, offices, and educational institutions. It provides detailed action plans aligned with the unique environmental needs of the region, ensuring that communities and institutions can adopt the most effective and relevant sustainability practices.

- **Community Engagement & Collaboration**

EcoValence orchestrates region-specific community engagement and collaborative initiatives within the 10 to 1500 km² expanse. It unites local authorities, industries, offices, and educational institutions through challenges and eco-conscious behaviors, fostering collective impact. By promoting community-driven efforts, the app helps cultivate a sense of shared responsibility and collective action towards a more sustainable future.

- **Seamless Carbon Credit Integration**

EcoValence integrates with recognized carbon offset programs, supporting area-specific emissions mitigation initiatives. It enables institutions to track their local environmental efforts and contribute to verified projects aligning with their specific environmental impact. This seamless integration promotes accountability and incentivizes sustainable practices through tangible rewards.

- **Data Visualization and Reporting Tools**

The app offers visual representations of carbon footprint data and collective sustainability progress. It provides charts, graphs, and reports illustrating individual and collective environmental impact within the designated region. These visualization tools help users track their progress and understand the effectiveness of their sustainability initiatives.

- **Collaboration Tools for Institutions and Governments**

EcoValence facilitates collaborative efforts among local governments, industries, offices, and educational institutions within the specified geographical area. It encourages the exchange of best practices and coordinated initiatives towards sustainability. By fostering cooperation and shared learning, the app helps accelerate the adoption of sustainable practices.

- **Notification and Alert Systems**

The app sends alerts and notifications about environmental news, policy changes, upcoming challenges and community initiatives pertinent to the specific region size. This feature keeps users informed and engaged in ongoing sustainability efforts, ensuring they are up-to-date with relevant information and opportunities for involvement.

- **Benchmarking and Comparative Analysis**

EcoValence provides benchmarking tools and comparative analysis features, enabling entities to measure their environmental progress against regional standards and best practices. This encourages healthy competition and goal-setting for continuous improvement. By understanding where they stand relative to others, communities and institutions can set realistic and ambitious targets, fostering a culture of sustainability and continuous advancement.

- **Resource Allocation Recommendations**

The app offers recommendations for optimized resource allocation, suggesting efficient utilization of energy, water, and waste management techniques specific to the area. These insights assist in resource conservation and efficiency enhancement across different sectors.

- **Ecosystem Health Monitoring**

Monitors the health and resilience of local ecosystems, offering insights into biodiversity, habitat preservation, and measures to restore ecological balance. This empowers decision-makers to take proactive steps for ecosystem conservation and restoration, ensuring that natural habitats are protected and rejuvenated.

- **Tailored Educational Modules**

The app provides tailored educational modules and training materials focused on environmental awareness and sustainability practices relevant to the region. These resources empower individuals and institutions with knowledge for informed decision-making and proactive environmental actions.

- **Stakeholder Engagement Forums**

EcoValence establishes online forums and discussion platforms encouraging stakeholder engagement, and fostering dialogue, idea sharing, and collaboration among entities within the region. This creates a unified space for knowledge exchange and collective problem-solving.

- **Long-term Impact Measurement**

The app tracks and measures the long-term impact of sustainability initiatives implemented within the region, providing insights into the efficacy of various strategies. This helps in adapting and refining approaches for sustained positive environmental outcomes.

This comprehensive suite of tools and resources tailored to specific geographical areas empowers communities and institutions, fostering collective responsibility and meaningful strides towards sustainable living across various sectors.

How the App Works

Sign-up and Area Selection

Upon registering on EcoValence, users choose their specific geographical area ranging from

10 to 1500 sq. km. This selection ensures that their actions and contributions are aligned with the environmental concerns and efforts within their community or institution's location.

Calculate Your Carbon Footprint

EcoValence features an adaptive carbon footprint calculator that helps users assess their environmental impact based on the following factors:

- **Transportation:** Users input information about the transportation modes predominantly used in the designated area, whether it's public transport, private vehicles, cycling, or walking. This helps in assessing the impact of transportation-related emissions.

- **Energy Consumption:** Users provide information is provided about the primary sources of energy used within the area, such as solar power, fossil fuels, wind energy, etc., to gauge the environmental impact of energy consumption.

- **Waste Generation:** Details about recycling programs, waste disposal methods, and other waste reduction initiatives occurring in the area are provided to understand and mitigate the impact of waste generation.

- **Operational Practices:** Users describe the area's energy usage patterns, waste management strategies, and existing sustainability efforts. This information aids in comprehensively assessing the overall environmental impact of day-to-day operations within the specified region.

Personalized Sustainability Plans

Users receive customized plans containing actionable steps and strategies specifically tailored to reduce the carbon footprint of the designated area. These plans offer practical recommendations for implementing sustainable practices within the community or institution, aiming for tangible environmental improvements.

Join Forces

EcoValence encourages users to actively participate in area-specific challenges and collaborative initiatives along with neighbors, local organizations, and relevant entities within the region. This collective engagement fosters a sense of shared responsibility and encourages concerted efforts toward achieving common sustainability goals.

Learn with Ease

The app provides accessible and user-friendly resources, such as articles, videos, and tips, offering insights into local environmental science and practical sustainable living practices. This knowledge empowers users with information to make informed decisions and take proactive environmental actions.

Rewards for Going Green

Users are incentivized for their sustainable actions by earning credits based on implemented eco-friendly practices and support provided to verified emission reduction projects. These credits act as a tangible acknowledgement and encouragement for active participation in sustainable initiatives.

Support Verified Environmental Projects

The earned credits can be utilized to contribute to certified environmental projects within the specific area. This system directly encourages and supports local sustainability efforts by allocating credits to initiatives aimed at reducing emissions and enhancing environmental conservation.

Track Progress Visually

Interactive charts and graphs visualize both individual and collective environmental contributions within the designated area. This visual representation allows users to track and understand the impact of their actions, fostering a sense of accountability and motivation for continued involvement.

Connect for Collective Impact

The app serves as a platform for collaboration, facilitating engagement and information-sharing among local entities. Users can share insights, exchange ideas, and work collectively towards common sustainability objectives within the area.

Stay Informed and Get Assistance

Users receive timely updates on environmental news, policy changes, and relevant information about the specific region. Additionally, customer support is readily available within the app to provide guidance and assistance whenever needed, ensuring a smooth user experience.

These enhanced functionalities ensure a comprehensive and tailored experience for users across various sizes of designated regions while actively engaging them in reducing their carbon footprint and supporting sustainability initiatives through the integrated carbon credit system. This comprehensive process enables users to actively contribute to environmental sustainability within their designated area, fostering a sense of responsibility, community involvement, and continuous progress towards a greener future.

Revenue Model and Sustainability

Subscription revenue forms the financial backbone of EcoValence, supporting ongoing app development, feature enhancements, and data analysis, all while driving the sustainability mission forward. Subscription plans are designed to accommodate diverse user needs, offering a user-friendly interface, regular updates, and valuable insights to drive lasting environmental change. EcoValence provides various membership tiers for users, institutions and businesses within specific geographic zones each offering access to tools, data, and specialized features to encourage sustainable practices. Here's how its revenue model aligns with sustainability:

- **Subscription Plans:** Offers different levels of access to EcoValence's features for users, institutions, or businesses within specific geographic areas. People can choose from various subscription packages, each providing different benefits or more advanced tools within the app.

- **Free Basic Version, Paid Upgrades:** Gives users a basic version of the app for free, allowing access to essential functions. Then, offer premium features or advanced tools as paid upgrades or part of a subscription package.

- **Partnerships and Sponsorships:** Collaborating with eco-conscious brands and organizations fosters sustainability by promoting shared values. These partnerships can fund app development, features, or educational content, supporting EcoValence's mission while expanding its reach.

- **Carbon Credit Transactions:** Facilitating carbon credit transactions encourages users to engage in eco-friendly actions. The revenue generated from transaction fees sustains the app's operations while contributing to environmental projects aimed at offsetting carbon emissions.

- **Data Analytics Services:** Offer detailed data analysis and customized reports based on the environmental data collected within the app. Organizations, businesses, or local governments can pay for these insights to drive their sustainability initiatives.

- **Consulting Services:** Provide expert consultation on sustainability strategies and practices using the app's accumulated data. Charge a fee for personalized advice and guidance.

- **In-App Advertising:** Display relevant and unobtrusive ads within the app. These advertisements could promote eco-friendly products or services, generating revenue through ad placements.

In essence, EcoValence's revenue model is designed to support its operational sustainability while simultaneously encouraging and facilitating eco-friendly behaviors. By leveraging partnerships, data insights, and user engagement, the app promotes sustainability not only through its functionalities but also through its revenue-generating avenues.

Conclusion

By nurturing a sense of community ownership, offering insightful resources, and fostering collaboration, EcoValence goes beyond being a mere application. It becomes a catalyst for collective empowerment, inspiring individuals and entities to embrace and champion environmentally conscious behaviors within their designated regions.

In a nutshell, EcoValence transcends its digital realm, embodying a philosophy of unity and change, steering communities and institutions towards a symbiotic relationship with the environment. It stands as an instrument of progress towards a sustainable future where responsible actions today pave the way for a thriving planet tomorrow.

Chapter-14

Pain Points

Introduction

The world is changing rapidly, presenting us with a range of pressing challenges that are often overlooked. These challenges spanning environmental, social, and technological fields, also offer substantial opportunities for groundbreaking transformation. This chapter explores sustainable startup ideas that address these neglected issues to providing innovate solutions and fresh perspectives. By outlining such issues effectively here today - it's hoped readers will feel more inspired towards action & awareness within their communities or beyond so they can become active contributors toward meaningful progress going forward!

1. Rain Water Harvesting in Societies

Lack of Awareness and Education

Many residents may lack awareness regarding the importance and benefits of rainwater harvesting. Without adequate education and outreach programs, there's limited knowledge about the techniques, advantages, and feasibility of rainwater harvesting. This lack of information results in hesitation or reluctance among communities to invest time and resources into implementing such systems.

Infrastructure and Cost Constraints

Implementing rainwater harvesting systems often requires a considerable upfront investment. The cost associated with installing infrastructure such as collection tanks, pipelines, and filtration systems can be prohibitive for many societies. Additionally, some societies might lack suitable infrastructure or available space to set up these systems, further hindering their implementation.

Maintenance Challenge

Effective maintenance is crucial for the proper functioning of rainwater harvesting infrastructure. However, due to limited knowledge or expertise among residents, ensuring regular maintenance can be challenging. Lack of financial resources or easy access to maintenance services can also contribute to the neglect of these systems, leading to inefficiencies or malfunctions.

Regulatory and Policy Issues

Clear and supportive policies and regulations play a pivotal role in encouraging rainwater harvesting adoption. However, the absence of specific regulations or incentives from local governing bodies may result in a lack of motivation or obligation for societies to embrace these systems. Unclear guidelines or compliance requirements may add further complexity to the process.

Perception and Social Acceptance

Traditional methods of water sourcing might be deeply ingrained in the community, leading to skepticism or resistance towards rainwater harvesting. Some residents may perceive it as an inconvenience or doubt its effectiveness compared to conventional water sources. Overcoming these social perceptions and fostering acceptance becomes a significant challenge.

Addressing these challenges requires a multi-faceted approach involving educational campaigns, policy advocacy, technical support, and financial incentives. Efforts aimed at raising awareness, providing financial aid or subsidies, ensuring clear regulations, and offering technical guidance can encourage wider adoption of rainwater harvesting practices in societies.

2. Water Logging in Urban Areas

Inadequate Drainage Infrastructure

Many urban areas lack proper drainage systems capable of efficiently channeling excess rainwater. Outdated or insufficient drainage infrastructure leads to water accumulation on streets, sidewalks, and residential areas, causing frequent waterlogging during heavy rainfall.

Urban Development and Land Use Changes

Rapid urbanization often results in the concretization of surfaces through roads, pavements, and buildings. This impervious surface prevents rainwater from being absorbed into the ground, exacerbating runoff. Improper planning and unchecked construction further contribute to increased surface water runoff, leading to waterlogging in low-lying areas.

Climate Change and Extreme Weather Events

Changing weather patterns intensify rainfall, and more frequent extreme weather events due to climate change pose significant challenges. Urban areas are often ill-prepared to handle sudden deluges, resulting in inundation and waterlogging.

Lack of Maintenance and Cleanliness

Inadequate maintenance and regular cleaning of drains, culverts, and stormwater drains contribute to waterlogging issues. Negligence in clearing debris and waste from these systems hampers water flow and deepens waterlogging problems.

Encroachment and Illegal Construction

Encroachment onto natural drainage channels, such as riverbanks or wetlands, and illegal construction in flood-prone areas further aggravate waterlogging issues. These unauthorized structures obstruct the natural flow of water, leading to localized flooding and water accumulation.

Improper Urban Planning and Governance

Inadequate urban planning, poor zoning regulations, and weak land use policies often overlook the importance of proper drainage systems. Weak governance, inadequate enforcement of building codes, and a lack of long-term urban development strategies contribute to waterlogging problems in cities.

Addressing waterlogging in urban areas necessitates comprehensive urban planning, infrastructure development, and policy implementation. This includes investing in better drainage systems, regular maintenance, sustainable urban design, and stricter enforcement of regulations to mitigate the impact of waterlogging during heavy rainfall and ensure the resilience of urban areas against flooding.

3. Commercialized IIT JEE Coaching vs. Lack of Merit Based, Low-Fee Classes for Deserving Students

Financial Barrier

Commercial coaching classes for IIT JEE often charge exorbitant fees, creating a significant financial burden for many aspirants. These high costs are unaffordable for students from economically weaker backgrounds, limiting their access to quality education.

Quality Discrepancy

While commercial coaching centres offer comprehensive study materials and expert guidance, the quality of education might not always justify the high fees. Conversely, the lack of affordable, merit-based coaching often results in students receiving subpar or inadequate preparation.

Merit-Based Opportunities

Deserving students who cannot afford expensive coaching classes might miss out on achieving their potential due to the unavailability of merit-based, low-fee coaching options. This lack of accessibility limits opportunities for talented individuals to excel in competitive exams like the IIT JEE.

Social and Economic Divide

The prevalence of expensive coaching classes widens the gap between students from privileged backgrounds and those with financial constraints. This perpetuates social and economic inequalities, as quality education becomes a privilege limited to those who can afford it.

Pressure and Stress on Students

The competitive nature of IIT JEE exams coupled with the scarcity of affordable coaching creates immense pressure on students. They might feel compelled to opt for high-cost coaching, leading to stress and anxiety, affecting their mental health and well-being.

Dependence on Private Coaching

The over-reliance on private coaching centres for IIT JEE preparation marginalizes students who might excel through self-study or require alternative, affordable coaching methods tailored to their learning needs.

Lack of Government Initiatives

There is a notable absence of government-supported initiatives providing quality, affordable coaching specifically designed for deserving students aspiring to crack competitive exams like the IIT JEE.

Addressing these challenges entails the development of merit-based coaching programs subsidized by the government or educational institutions. Initiatives focusing on providing comprehensive, high-quality coaching at affordable rates or free of cost could level the playing field, offering equal opportunities to students from diverse socio-economic backgrounds. Additionally, advocacy for inclusive educational policies that reduce dependence on expensive coaching classes while ensuring quality learning resources is essential to bridge this gap in the education sector.

4. Reuse of Old & Used Text Books, Lab Equipment, Stationery and Laptop Computers by Students in Schools

Limited Access to Resources

Many students, especially in economically disadvantaged areas, lack access to new educational materials due to financial constraints, making it difficult for them to keep up with their studies.

High Cost of New Material

The cost of purchasing new textbooks, lab equipment, stationery, and laptops can be prohibitive for many families, leading to a situation where students may not have the necessary resources for effective learning.

Environmental Impact

Producing new educational materials requires substantial resources and contributes to environmental degradation. Encouraging reuse reduces the demand for new production and minimizes waste generation.

Obsolete or Outdated Materials

Some reused materials might be outdated or not aligned with the current curriculum, potentially hindering students' learning experiences.

Quality and Condition

Reused materials may not always be in good condition, impacting their usability and effectiveness for learning purposes.

Stigma Around Used Materials

Some students may face stigma or embarrassment when using visibly used or older materials, impacting their confidence and self-esteem.

Lack of a Systematic Approach

Schools and educational institutions may lack a structured system or platform for efficiently redistributing and reusing educational resources, making it challenging to organize such initiatives.

Hygiene and Sanitation Concerns

Used materials, especially items like stationery or equipment, may not undergo proper sanitation processes, potentially raising hygiene concerns among students.

Limited Subject Coverage

The availability of reused textbooks and educational resources might be limited to popular or mainstream subjects, leaving students studying niche or specialized subjects with fewer options.

Teacher Adaptation

Teachers might need to adapt their teaching methods or lesson plans to accommodate varied resources, potentially requiring additional effort and time.

Administration and Inventory Management

Managing and maintaining an inventory of reused educational materials can be a logistical challenge for educational institutions, requiring efficient administration and tracking systems.

Copyright and Licensing Issues

There could be legal complexities related to copyright or licensing when redistributing or reusing certain educational materials, requiring proper permissions or agreements.

Perception of Quality

There might be a perception among students or parents that reused materials are of inferior quality compared to new ones, affecting their willingness to adopt such resources.

Addressing these challenges may involve implementing comprehensive policies, collaborating with publishers and educational content providers to facilitate access to updated materials, investing in refurbishing and sanitization processes, and fostering a culture that values the environmental and economic benefits of reusing educational resources. Additionally, building partnerships with organizations specializing in resource redistribution and recycling could help create sustainable solutions for educational material reuse.

5. Digital Detoxification
Digital Addiction

Without digital detox initiatives, individuals may develop addictive behaviors toward digital devices and platforms, leading to excessive screen time, decreased productivity, and potential health issues associated with prolonged use.

Mental Health Concerns

Excessive use of digital devices, social media, and online platforms without breaks can contribute to mental health issues such as anxiety, depression, and stress. The absence of detox measures may intensify these problems.

Physical Health Impacts

Prolonged screen time and sedentary behavior due to digital dependency can lead to physical health issues like eye strain, headaches, poor posture, and disrupted sleep patterns.

Reduced Social Interaction

Excessive use of digital devices may lead to reduced face-to-face social interaction, impacting personal relationships and social skills development.

Decline in Productivity

Constant connectivity without breaks can lead to reduced focus, attention span, and productivity, affecting work performance and overall efficiency.

Impact on Well-being

Without dedicated detox strategies, individuals may struggle to find a balance between their digital and real-world lives, leading to a decreased sense of well-being and fulfilment.

Negative Impact on Relationships

Overuse of digital devices can strain relationships, causing misunderstandings, reduced communication, and emotional disconnect among family members, friends, and partners.

Inability to Disconnect

The lack of structured digital detoxification methods can make it challenging for individuals to disconnect from the digital world, leading to an 'always-on' mentality that can cause burnout and fatigue.

Overwhelming Information Overload

The constant influx of digital information without adequate breaks can overwhelm individuals, impairing their ability to process information effectively and make sound decisions.

Decreased Focus and Attention

Continuous exposure to digital stimuli without breaks can lead to decreased concentration, making it difficult to focus on tasks and complete them efficiently.

Implementing digital detoxification initiatives can help alleviate these pain points by promoting healthier relationships with technology, encouraging breaks from digital devices, and fostering a more balanced lifestyle that prioritizes mental and physical well-being.

6. Recyclable Single-Use Plastics Alternatives

Limited Options

The available alternatives to single-use plastics might be limited, making it challenging for businesses and consumers to find suitable replacements for various applications such as packaging, utensils, or containers.

Cost Constraints

Environmentally friendly alternatives might be more expensive to produce, purchase, or implement than traditional single-use plastics, posing financial challenges for businesses and consumers, especially in mass production.

Performance and Durability

Some alternatives may lack the durability or performance standards of plastics, affecting the shelf life, usability, or quality of the products, thereby impacting consumer satisfaction.

Lack of Infrastructure

Inadequate infrastructure for collecting, recycling, or composting alternative materials might exist, making it difficult to properly dispose of or recycle these materials, potentially negating their environmental benefits.

Consumer Behavior and Acceptance

Changing consumer behavior and preferences towards these alternatives can be challenging, as people might be accustomed to the convenience and familiarity of single-use plastics.

Regulatory Hurdles

Regulatory frameworks might not be in place to incentivize or mandate the use of recyclable alternatives, making it challenging for businesses to transition away from traditional plastics.

Supply Chain Challenges

Sourcing raw materials, manufacturing, and distribution of alternative products could pose logistical challenges in the supply chain, impacting availability and affordability.

Product Adaptability

Some alternative materials might not be suitable for all applications or industries, limiting their usage in certain sectors or products.

Addressing these pain points is crucial to encourage the adoption of recyclable alternatives to single-use plastics, necessitating innovation, investment, and collaboration among various stakeholders across industries and governments.

7. Mental Health Solutions for Remote Workers

Social Isolation

Remote work can lead to feelings of isolation and loneliness due to the lack of in-person interactions with colleagues, impacting mental well-being and contributing to depression or anxiety.

Blurred Work-Life Boundaries

Difficulty in separating work life from personal life can lead to increased stress, burnout, and reduced productivity as remote workers often find themselves working longer hours or being always 'on.'

Limited Access to Support Services

Remote workers might have limited access to mental health support services or resources, including in-person therapy, counselling, or company-sponsored mental health programs typically available in traditional office settings.

Communication Challenges

Over-reliance on digital communication tools may lead to miscommunication, misunderstandings, or feeling disconnected from the team, adding to stress and anxiety.

Technological Issues

Connectivity issues, software problems, or inadequate technological support can alleviate stress and frustration, impacting mental health and overall job satisfaction.

Ergonomic Challenges

Poor ergonomics in-home workspaces might lead to physical discomfort, which can contribute to mental stress and decreased productivity.

Time Zone Differences

Collaborating with colleagues or clients across different time zones may lead to irregular hours or attending meetings during non-traditional working hours, disrupting sleep patterns and causing stress.

Performance Pressure

Remote workers may feel pressured to overperform or constantly prove their productivity due to the lack of physical presence, leading to stress, anxiety, and decreased job satisfaction.

Career Growth Concerns

Limited visibility or opportunities for career advancement and networking due to physical separation from the workplace may cause anxiety or feelings of stagnation among remote workers.

Financial Insecurities

Contract-based or freelance remote work can bring uncertainty about income stability or job security, leading to stress and mental health challenges.

Remote Onboarding and Integration

Starting a new remote job can be challenging as it might lack the camaraderie and integration opportunities of an in-person workplace, potentially causing feelings of isolation and stress in new hires.

Addressing these pain points requires a combination of supportive company policies, access to mental health resources, effective communication strategies, work-life balance encouragement, and creating supportive remote work environments to promote positive mental health for remote workers.

8. Urban Air Quality Monitoring

Health Risks

Poor air quality in urban areas is linked to various health issues such as respiratory problems, allergies, cardiovascular diseases, and lung-related illnesses, impacting the overall well-being of residents.

Lack of Real-time Data Accessibility

Accessibility to real-time air quality data in certain urban areas might be limited or unavailable, making it challenging for individuals to make informed decisions about outdoor activities or necessary precautions.

Uneven Distribution of Monitoring Stations

In many urban regions, monitoring stations might be concentrated in certain areas, leading to disparities in data accuracy and representation across different neighborhoods.

Technological Limitations

The reliability and accuracy of some air quality monitoring devices could be questioned, affecting the credibility of the gathered data and hindering the effectiveness of pollution control measures.

Public Awareness and Understanding

There might be a lack of public awareness or understanding regarding the severity of air quality issues and their impact on health, which could hinder community-driven efforts for improvement.

Regulatory Compliance and Enforcement

Challenges might exist in enforcing regulations and standards related to air quality, impacting the implementation of measures to control pollution from various sources such as vehicles, industries, and construction sites.

Budget Constraints

Developing and maintaining an extensive air quality monitoring network involves significant costs, and budget constraints might limit the expansion or improvement of monitoring systems in some urban areas.

Data Interpretation and Communication

Even when data is available, it might be challenging for the general public to interpret complex air quality metrics, limiting their ability to take appropriate actions to protect their health.

Addressing these challenges might involve deploying advanced sensor technologies, enhancing data accessibility through user-friendly interfaces or apps, increasing public awareness, collaborating with local authorities for effective policies, and fostering community engagement to improve urban air quality.

9. Localized Water Purification Solutions

Limited Access to Clean Water

Many areas, particularly in remote or underprivileged regions, lack access to clean and safe drinking water due to inadequate purification facilities.

High Costs of Equipment

The initial cost of setting up localized water purification systems, such as filtration units or purification plants, can be prohibitively expensive for communities with limited financial resources.

Maintenance and Operation

Ensuring the consistent operation and maintenance of water purification systems may pose challenges due to the need for technical expertise, regular servicing, and spare parts, especially in areas with limited infrastructure.

Sustainability and Environmental Impact

Some water purification methods may be energy-intensive or require chemical treatments, raising concerns about sustainability and their impact on the environment.

Community Participation and Education

Engaging and educating local communities about the importance of clean water, proper usage of purification systems, and sustainable water practices is crucial but can be challenging.

Lack of Infrastructure

Remote or rural areas often lack the necessary infrastructure to support the installation and maintenance of water purification systems, including electricity and proper sanitation facilities.

Scalability and Capacity

Scaling up localized purification solutions to cater to larger populations or areas might pose logistical challenges, especially in emergencies or during sudden population surges.

Technological Suitability

Identifying the most suitable water purification technology for a specific area's water quality and requirements is crucial. Some technologies may not be efficient or effective in removing specific contaminants present in the water.

Behavioral Change

Encouraging behavior change regarding water usage, sanitation practices, and the importance of clean water consumption within communities can be a slow and challenging process.

Regulatory Barriers

Regulatory approvals and compliance with local laws and standards can sometimes delay or hinder the implementation of localized purification solutions.

Resolving these issues may involve the collaboration of various stakeholders, including governments, NGOs, technology innovators, and local communities, to ensure sustainable, affordable, and effective water purification solutions that address the unique challenges of each region.

10. Local Food Loop
Logistical Challenges

Coordinating the timely collection and redistribution of surplus or near-expiry food from restaurants and stores to local food banks or kitchens can be challenging due to logistical issues such as transportation, storage, and distribution.

Quality Control

Ensuring the quality and safety of surplus food items nearing expiration to be redirected for consumption requires meticulous inspection and monitoring, adding complexity to the process.

Regulatory Compliance

Adhering to food safety and health regulations while redistributing surplus food might involve legal complexities, especially concerning liability and compliance with food handling and storage guidelines.

Consumer Awareness

Educating consumers about the safety and reliability of redirected surplus food items is essential to encourage acceptance and usage, as there might be skepticism or misunderstanding regarding the quality of such items.

Wastage Reduction

Efficiently managing surplus food distribution to minimize waste and avoid instances of redirected food items going unused due to overestimation or improper handling.

Financial Sustainability

Establishing and maintaining a local food loop requires financial support for operational costs such as transportation, storage facilities, and staff, which may pose challenges in terms of sustainable funding.

Seasonal Variability

Seasonal changes and fluctuations in food supply might lead to challenges in consistently sourcing surplus or imperfect but edible food from local businesses.

Consumer Perception

Overcoming stigmas or biases associated with consuming surplus or near-expiry food items may pose a challenge, affecting public acceptance and participation in such initiatives.

Lack of Standardization

The absence of standardized processes and guidelines across different businesses or sectors for redistributing surplus food could hinder the seamless implementation of a local food loop.

Infrastructure Limitations

In areas with inadequate infrastructure, such as regions with limited access to refrigeration or storage facilities, maintaining the quality and safety of redistributed food items becomes more challenging.

Partnership Engagement

Encouraging active participation and engagement from local businesses, restaurants, and grocery stores to commit to redistributing surplus food consistently can be a hurdle, especially if they have concerns about additional costs or efforts.

Overcoming these challenges may involve developing comprehensive guidelines, fostering partnerships, leveraging technology for efficient logistics, and raising awareness to create a supportive ecosystem for sustainable surplus food redistribution within local communities.

11. Limited Quality and Brand Options for Men's Sandals

Limited Fashion Options

Men often face limited fashion choices compared to women, resulting in fewer trendy sandal options, affecting their ability to express personal style through footwear.

Inconsistent Sizing

Inaccurate or inconsistent sizing across brands and styles leads to confusion and difficulty for customers in finding the right fit, resulting in returns or dissatisfaction.

Seasonal Availability

Limited availability of men's sandals throughout the year, particularly in regions with extreme weather conditions, might restrict choices during specific seasons.

Lack of Sustainable Options

Many available sandals may not prioritize sustainable materials or eco-friendly manufacturing practices, which could deter environmentally conscious consumers.

Comfort and Support Issues

Some sandals may lack adequate cushioning, arch support, or ergonomic designs, resulting in discomfort, foot pain, or potential health issues for wearers.

Poor Online Experience

Limited or inaccurate information online about the sandals' materials, durability, or construction might affect consumers' trust and confidence in making online purchases.

Addressing these issues involves a focus on creating versatile designs, standardized sizing, better online product descriptions, sustainable manufacturing practices, and emphasizing comfort and support in product development.

12. Virtual Events and Experiences

Limited Connectivity

Without such platforms, people miss out on opportunities to connect virtually, hindering networking, professional collaborations, and social interactions that could lead to valuable connections and partnerships.

Reduced Engagement

Lacking these technologies decreases engagement levels during conferences, meetings, and social gatherings, resulting in passive participation rather than active involvement or contribution to discussions.

Geographical Barriers

Physical distance becomes a significant obstacle for individuals who are unable to attend events in person, leading to isolation and exclusion from important discussions or knowledge-sharing sessions.

Inefficient Communication

Without platforms catering to virtual events, communication among geographically dispersed teams, communities, or professionals becomes less efficient and more time-consuming.

Learning Opportunities Lost

Education, training, and learning opportunities that could be delivered through virtual events are limited or non-existent, depriving individuals of skill development or knowledge acquisition.

Business and Innovation Stagnation

The lack of virtual platforms for events hinders business growth opportunities, innovative collaborations, and the ability to showcase products or services in a broader market.

Missed Marketing and Branding Opportunities

Brands and businesses lose out on the chance to expand their reach and engage with a wider audience, impacting their marketing strategies and brand visibility.

Social and Emotional Disconnect:

The inability to virtually connect with peers, colleagues, or friends during social events can lead to a sense of disconnection, affecting morale and emotional well-being.

Exclusion of Diverse Perspectives

Without inclusive virtual event platforms, the diverse voices and perspectives of individuals from various backgrounds, regions, or cultures are excluded from important discussions and decisions.

By implementing platforms and technologies that enhance virtual event experiences can address these shortcomings. Such technologies foster better communication, facilitate networking, promote inclusivity, and enable remote collaboration, bridging geographical gaps and maximizing engagement opportunities.

13. Affordable Renewable Energy Solutions

High Energy Costs

Without accessible renewable energy solutions, consumers may continue to rely on traditional, often expensive, non-renewable energy sources, leading to higher energy bills for both residential and commercial users.

Environmental Impact

The reliance on non-renewable energy sources perpetuates environmental degradation, including air and water pollution, contributing to climate change and its associated negative effects.

Resource Depletion

Continued dependence on fossil fuels can lead to the depletion of finite natural resources, causing long-term scarcity and increased prices.

Energy Insecurity

Without a diversified energy portfolio, regions heavily reliant on non-renewable sources might experience energy shortages or disruptions due to supply chain issues or geopolitical conflicts.

Health Risks

Non-renewable energy sources are often linked to health hazards due to pollution, impacting the well-being of individuals living near power plants or areas with high energy consumption.

Economic Implications

The lack of affordable renewable energy solutions might hinder economic growth, as investment opportunities and potential job creation in the renewable energy sector could be missed.

Limited Innovation

A lack of focus on renewable energy solutions might stall technological advancements and innovations in the sector, hindering progress towards more sustainable energy sources.

Energy Inequality

Communities with limited access to renewable energy solutions might face greater disparities in accessing clean and sustainable energy, perpetuating socio-economic inequalities.

Global Energy Dependence

Relying solely on non-renewable energy sources may reinforce global energy dependence on specific regions or countries, leading to geopolitical tensions or conflicts over energy resources.

Addressing these pain points by fostering accessible and affordable renewable energy solutions is crucial for mitigating environmental degradation, reducing energy costs, and promoting sustainable development globally.

14. AI-Powered Wildlife Conservation

Increased Poaching Incidents

Lack of AI-powered anti-poaching technologies may lead to a rise in illegal wildlife trade and poaching incidents due to the difficulty in monitoring and protecting vulnerable species.

Habitat Destruction

Without AI-based habitat monitoring systems, conservationists may struggle to detect and prevent habitat destruction, leading to a loss of biodiversity and wildlife displacement.

Ineffective Conservation Strategies

The absence of AI-powered data analytics may hinder conservationists from efficiently analyzing large volumes of ecological data, resulting in less effective conservation strategies.

Slow Response to Threats

Without automated monitoring systems, conservationists may face challenges in detecting and responding swiftly to wildlife threats such as habitat encroachment, human-wildlife conflicts, or disease outbreaks.

Limited Resources Allocation

In the absence of AI-based predictive modelling, allocating resources for conservation efforts becomes less strategic, potentially leading to misdirected or insufficient resource distribution.

Human-Wildlife Conflict

Without AI-driven technologies for tracking and analyzing animal behavior patterns, managing and mitigating human-wildlife conflicts becomes more challenging, impacting both human populations and wildlife.

Loss of Endangered Species

The inability to accurately monitor and protect endangered species habitats could lead to a decline in their populations and eventual extinction.

Reduced Conservation Funding

Inadequate data-driven insights may result in a lack of evidence-based reports, potentially reducing funding and support for wildlife conservation initiatives.

Ecosystem Imbalance

Failure to implement AI-powered conservation strategies may disrupt the ecological balance, impacting the health of entire ecosystems and affecting other species within the environment.

Limited Scientific Research Opportunities

A lack of AI-driven data analysis may hinder scientific research opportunities, slowing down the discovery of new conservation methods and understanding of wildlife behavior.

Leveraging AI for wildlife conservation helps address these pain points by providing efficient monitoring, predictive analytics, and adaptive strategies necessary for effective conservation efforts and the preservation of biodiversity.

15. Personalized Genomic Services

Limited Understanding of Ancestry

The lack of access to personalized genomic services for ancestry exploration might prevent individuals from discovering their genetic lineage and cultural heritage, resulting in a missed opportunity to connect with their familial roots.

Generic Nutrition Advice

The absence of personalized nutrition plans based on genetic data might result in generic dietary recommendations that fail to consider an individual's unique nutritional needs, potentially impacting health and wellness goals.

Inaccurate Lifestyle Guidance

Without personalized lifestyle recommendations derived from genetic data, individuals might receive generalized advice that lacks specificity, hindering the effectiveness of lifestyle modifications.

Reduced Health Awareness

The absence of insights from personalized genomic services could lead to a lack of awareness about potential genetic predispositions to certain health conditions, and missing opportunities for proactive healthcare management.

Missed Opportunities in Health Optimization

Without tailored health recommendations based on genetic data, individuals may not fully capitalize on opportunities to optimize their health and well-being through personalized interventions.

Unaddressed Behavioral Patterns

Lack of insights from genetic-based lifestyle recommendations might result in unaddressed behavioral patterns or habits that could potentially impact an individual's health and quality of life.

Challenges in Disease Prevention

The absence of tailored insights into genetic predispositions might hinder individuals from taking preventive measures against specific hereditary diseases or conditions.

Ethical and Privacy Concerns

Utilization of personal genetic data for non-health-related purposes might raise concerns about privacy, data security, and ethical considerations regarding the use and protection of sensitive information.

Offering personalized genomic services beyond health, such as ancestry exploration, personalized nutrition plans, and lifestyle recommendations based on genetic data, could address these pain points by providing individuals with comprehensive insights to make informed decisions about their ancestry, lifestyle choices, and overall well-being. However, it's crucial to ensure ethical practices, data security, and privacy protection while implementing such services.

16. Drone-Based Emergency Response
Delayed Medical Assistance

The absence of drone-based emergency response could lead to delays in delivering critical medical supplies and aid to remote or disaster-stricken areas, affecting the timeliness of emergency medical care.

Increased Risk of Fatalities

Without quick access to medical supplies or essential communication devices via drone delivery, individuals in remote areas facing emergencies may experience prolonged wait times, potentially leading to higher fatality rates.

Logistical Challenges in Disaster Relief

The absence of drone-based systems for emergency response could complicate disaster relief efforts, particularly in hard-to-reach or inaccessible areas, resulting in logistical bottlenecks and delays in aid distribution.

Limited Connectivity in Remote Regions

Remote areas might lack proper communication infrastructure, hindering the transmission of critical information and coordination of relief efforts during emergencies.

Inadequate Disaster Preparedness

Without a drone-based emergency response system, regions prone to disasters might be ill-prepared to handle urgent situations effectively, leading to chaos and disorganization during crises.

Dependency on Conventional Transport

Reliance solely on conventional transport methods (e.g., ground vehicles or air ambulances) for emergency supplies and aid may limit accessibility to remote or disaster-affected areas due to geographical constraints or roadblocks.

Escalating Humanitarian Crisis

Delayed response and limited access to essential supplies could worsen humanitarian crises in disaster-stricken regions, leading to a deterioration of living conditions and an increase in casualties.

Limitations in Resource Distribution

Without the agility and versatility of drone-based delivery systems, equitable distribution of resources, including medical supplies and aid, might be uneven or insufficient across affected areas.

Costly and Inefficient Operations

Traditional emergency response methods might be costlier and less efficient, especially in reaching remote areas or locations with damaged infrastructure, resulting in prolonged recovery periods.

Implementing a drone-based emergency response system can significantly alleviate these pain points by facilitating rapid, targeted, and efficient delivery of essential supplies, medical aid, and communication devices to remote or disaster-stricken areas, thereby saving lives, reducing response times, and enhancing disaster management capabilities.

17. Smart Waste Sorting Bins

Inefficient Waste Sorting

Without smart waste bins, manual waste sorting becomes the norm. This manual process can be time-consuming, labor-intensive, and prone to errors, leading to improper segregation of recyclables from general waste.

Contamination of Recyclables

Lack of proper sorting mechanisms can result in the contamination of recyclable materials with non-recyclables, diminishing the quality and value of the recycled materials and making them less desirable for recycling facilities.

Increased Landfill Waste

Inadequate segregation of recyclables from general waste leads to higher quantities of waste ending up in landfills. This contributes to environmental pollution, higher landfill usage, and limited space for waste disposal.

Resource Wastage

The absence of efficient waste sorting technologies leads to the squandering of valuable resources that could otherwise be recycled or repurposed, thereby contributing to resource depletion.

Environmental Impact

Improper waste disposal practices due to the lack of smart waste bins can lead to environmental pollution, harming ecosystems, soil, water bodies, and wildlife due to non-biodegradable or hazardous materials ending up in landfills or natural habitats.

High Processing Costs

Manual sorting of recyclables adds to operational costs for waste management facilities. These expenses are typically higher due to increased labor requirements and the need for advanced sorting technologies.

Limited Consumer Awareness

In the absence of smart waste bins that facilitate proper waste segregation, there's a lack of awareness among consumers regarding the importance of recycling and the need for responsible waste disposal practices.

Missed Opportunities for Upcycling

Without proper sorting, valuable materials that could be upcycled or repurposed for various products or industries are lost, resulting in missed opportunities for creating new goods from recycled materials.

Regulatory Compliance Issues

In regions with stringent waste management regulations, the absence of efficient waste sorting methods might lead to non-compliance issues, penalties, or fines for municipalities or waste management entities.

Implementing smart waste bins equipped with sensors and AI for automatic waste sorting can significantly address these pain points by promoting proper waste disposal, increasing recycling rates, reducing environmental impact, optimizing resource utilization, and enhancing the efficiency of waste management practices.

18. Lack of Urban Vertical Farming Co-Working Spaces (UVFCS)

Lack of Green Spaces in Urban Areas

As cities expand, green spaces diminish. Professionals often find themselves surrounded by concrete and glass, disconnected from nature. The absence of greenery affects mental well-being, creativity, and overall productivity.

Monotonous Work Environments

Traditional offices can be sterile and uninspiring. The same beige walls, fluorescent lighting, and cubicles can stifle creativity and reduce motivation.

Disconnect from Food Sources

In urban settings, people often lose touch with where their food comes from. Supermarkets and delivery apps provide convenience, but the origin of produce remains distant.

Health and Well-Being Challenges

Sedentary office jobs contribute to health issues—back pain, eye strain, and stress-related ailments. Lunch breaks are often rushed, leading to unhealthy eating habits.

19. Elderly Companion Robots

Loneliness and Isolation

Elderly individuals, especially those living alone or in care facilities, might experience heightened loneliness and isolation without a companion robot to interact with and provide companionship.

Limited Assistance with Daily Tasks

Elderly individuals often require assistance with everyday tasks. Without companion robots, they may struggle to receive immediate help for tasks such as medication reminders, fetching items, or mobility assistance.

Emotional Support Deficiency

Lack of emotional support might impact the mental health of the elderly. Companion robots, equipped with emotional intelligence, can offer comfort and much needed emotional support, filling the gap in their social environment.

Decreased Cognitive Stimulation

Interaction with companion robots that incorporate AI and cognitive engagement features can stimulate the cognitive abilities of the elderly. Without this interaction, there might be a decline in mental stimulation and cognitive health.

Safety Concerns

Companion robots can enhance safety of elderly by monitoring their well-being, detecting falls, or alerting caregivers in case of emergencies. Without this technology, the risk of accidents or health emergencies increases, especially for those living alone.

Increased Caregiver Burden

Without companion robots to assist in daily tasks and provide companionship, the burden on family members or professional caregivers might significantly increase, impacting their ability to balance caregiving responsibilities.

Limited Social Engagement

Elderly individuals may have limited opportunities for social interaction. Companion robots can serve as a means of facilitating social engagement, which otherwise might be lacking.

Dependence on Human Assistance

Without companion robots, elderly individuals might become overly dependent on human assistance for various tasks, reducing their sense of independence and autonomy.

Technology Divide

Lack of access to companion robots might amplify the digital divide among the elderly, leading to exclusion from the benefits of technological advancements in caregiving and companionship.

Unmet Emotional Needs

Elderly individuals often experience unmet emotional needs due to a lack of familial or social support. Companion robots can address these needs by providing consistent companionship and emotional support.

Developing companion robots designed for the elderly, integrating AI and emotional intelligence, can significantly mitigate these pain points by offering companionship, assistance, safety monitoring, and emotional support to enhance the well-being and quality of life of the elderly population.

Milton Keynes UK
Ingram Content Group UK Ltd.
UKHW021121201124
451264UK00017B/327

9 789364 526258